T0358239

Cambridge Elements ☰

Elements in Applied Linguistics
edited by
Li Wei
University College London
Zhu Hua
University College London

NARRATIVE AND RELIGION IN THE SUPERDIVERSE CITY

Stephen Pihlaja
Aston University

CAMBRIDGE
UNIVERSITY PRESS

Shaftesbury Road, Cambridge CB2 8EA, United Kingdom

One Liberty Plaza, 20th Floor, New York, NY 10006, USA

477 Williamstown Road, Port Melbourne, VIC 3207, Australia

314–321, 3rd Floor, Plot 3, Splendor Forum, Jasola District Centre,
New Delhi – 110025, India

103 Penang Road, #05–06/07, Visioncrest Commercial, Singapore 238467

Cambridge University Press is part of Cambridge University Press & Assessment,
a department of the University of Cambridge.

We share the University's mission to contribute to society through the pursuit of
education, learning and research at the highest international levels of excellence.

www.cambridge.org
Information on this title: www.cambridge.org/9781009475983

DOI: 10.1017/9781009406994

First published 2024

A catalogue record for this publication is available from the British Library.

ISBN 978-1-009-47598-3 Hardback
ISBN 978-1-009-40698-7 Paperback
ISSN 2633-5069 (online)
ISSN 2633-5050 (print)

Cambridge University Press & Assessment has no responsibility for the persistence
or accuracy of URLs for external or third-party internet websites referred to in this
publication and does not guarantee that any content on such websites is, or will
remain, accurate or appropriate.

Narrative and Religion in the Superdiverse City

Elements in Applied Linguistics

DOI: 10.1017/9781009406994
First published online: May 2024

Stephen Pihlaja
Aston University
Author for correspondence: Stephen Pihlaja, s.pihlaja@aston.ac.uk

Abstract: This Element focuses on how narrative is used to construct religious identity in superdiverse contexts, considering specifically how people talk about their own religious identity and the religious identity of others. Drawing on interviews with twenty-five participants and numerous site visits throughout the city of Birmingham (UK), the analysis focuses on how self and other positioning is used to construct religious identity in talk about beliefs, actions, and behaviours in different contexts. Additionally, the analysis shows how conflict emerges and is resolved in spaces where people of different faiths and no faith interact, and how people talk about and understand community. Finally, a model for talking about faith in diverse contexts is presented to help people find common goals and act together in working towards shared interests.

Keywords: superdiversity, religion, citizenship, racism, narrative

ISBNs: 9781009475983 (HB), 9781009406987 (PB), 9781009406994 (OC)
ISSNs: 2633-5069 (online), 2633-5050 (print)

Contents

Background

For many years, narratives about changing demographics in urban areas like Birmingham have been an ongoing part of media coverage in the UK. Birmingham, the 2020 census confirmed, has become a white minority city, with more and more young people coming from historically minoritised communities (Jackson, 2018). So-called superdiverse (Vertovec, 2007) communities include migrants, both recent and with longer-standing connections to the UK, with people of different ethnicities and different cultural traditions, languages, and religious identities. For many, the lived experience of superdiversity is a positive one, with community organisations working together to improve the lives of everyone in the city. However, migrants in the UK and around the world are frequently the subject of negative stories which are fuelled by and feed into prejudice, misunderstanding, and discrimination. Particularly in reporting on Muslim communities, minority religious identity can be felt, particularly among young people, as one way they are othered in society (Thompson & Pihlaja, 2017). At the same time, research into linguistic superdiversity has shown that the media narratives of segregated communities living in an isolated way are erroneous (see, for example, previous work on linguistic diversity in Birmingham: Blackledge & Creese, 2020; Creese & Blackledge, 2019).

This Element therefore investigates narratives about religious identity in superdiverse contexts and aims to understand how people of different faiths see themselves in daily life where they regularly interact with people of different faiths and no faith. Through looking carefully at how people tell stories about their experiences, the Element will show how ways of talking about religious superdiversity emerge from people's experiences in the city, and how living with people of different faiths and no faith creates a context for people to recognise and appreciate shared values and work together for common goals. In the first section, I review the current state of research in religion and discourse, how religious identity and language have been investigated in the past, and how religious identity has been understood from different disciplinary perspectives.

Religious identity can be an important part of how people view themselves and understand their place in the social world. Like other parts of identity, it is often viewed, particularly among religious believers, as a relatively settled part of who a person is, not something that shifts from moment to moment. When changes in belief do occur, they can be embedded in stories about conversion, where a person can clearly and specifically recount how their thinking about the world shifted and the causes for it (Hanks, 2013; Inge, 2016). At the same time, in the contemporary world, more and more people have come to have less fixed understandings of their own religious belief and identity. The category of 'spiritual, but not religious' has grown in popularity, even among people who might also ascribe to a specific, named faith category (Ammerman, 2013). Moreover, religious identity can be linked to cultural, ethnic, and/or national identities, where being a member of a religion is understood to be an important part of what it means to be another ethnic or national category. The relationship between 'culture' and 'religion' can be difficult to articulate as separate from one another, particularly in diasporic contexts of religious minorities in Europe (Fadil, 2017; Gholami, 2015, 2017). This is not, however, to downplay the importance of belief and faith religious identity, something that differs in importance depending on the religious belief or individual in question.

Understanding one's individual identity is closely related to an understanding of one's own community. And knowledge of what it means to be a member of that community requires information on how it is similar or different from other communities, a key principle of social identity theory (Abrams & Hogg, 2010; Hogg, 2004; Tajfel, 1983). Differentiating people and communities can be achieved linguistically using group categories and labels, and the importance of categorisation in understanding self and others has been of interest in linguistics, most notably in membership categorisation analysis, first proposed by Sacks (1992) and later developed by others (Housley & Fitzgerald, 2002). Categories and labels necessarily exist in a dynamic context. 'Christian' or 'Muslim' or 'Buddhist' will mean different things in different contexts and times, depending on who is speaking to whom and what is most prominent in a society at any given time. Because of this, even people from the same religious category might disagree about what it means exactly to be a member of that category (Pihlaja, 2014).

The role of discourse in the construction of identity has been a key focus of sociolinguistic, conversation analytic, and narrative research, and the relationship between language and identity has long been a focus of sociolinguistics and psycholinguistics (Ringrow, 2021). However, the role of religion in identity and language has had less focus in sociolinguistics. There has instead been more interest in religion as it relates to relationships among ethnic, national, and linguistic identities (Lytra et al., 2016; Omoniyi & Fishman, 2006) and various studies have looked at how religious identity links with ethnicity, place, and gender, seeing religion not merely as a set of beliefs and practices but as an essential part of culture and an essential practice for many people (Lytra et al., 2016). Sierra's (2023) work, for example, showed how several different identities – Jewish, a New York resident, and an actor – emerged in discourse, with religious identity being one part of who someone is. Ringrow's (2020b) work also examined different intersections in identities, examining discussion of motherhood and religious belief in technologically mediated contexts. The study showed the ways these factors influence how people talk about their experiences and how common ways of talking about experience emerge.

More broadly, interest in the relationship between language and religion has occasionally been an area of interest. Van Noppen (1981, 2006), building on previous work done by others such as Crystal (1965), looked at how religious or sacred language was unique compared to other kinds of 'everyday' language. Similar treatment of religious language as unique can be seen in research that examined relationships between how people understand and act in religious settings (Soskice, 1985, 2007; Yelle et al., 2019), as well as how language is used in religious communities for communicating about the sacred and leading to a sense of community and shared identity. 'Religious language', broadly understood, can be a substantial part of how a language is spoken, for example, in how 'Allah phrases' like *mashallah* (what God has willed has happened) and *inshallah* (if God wills it) become a part of everyday conversations in Arabic (Clift & Helani, 2010) or how Evangelical Christians reference hymns and scripture in their interactions (Hobbs, 2020; van Noppen, 2012). Rosowsky (2019) has also shown how 'sacred languages' can be a part of dynamic language use in superdiverse contexts, where different languages are being used among pupils in faith-based supplementary schools. This research into religious and sacred language has generally seen it as something that can be identified in talk, either in its function or its intertextual relationship to sacred or other religious texts. In linguistic anthropology, Bhatt and Wang (2023) have explored how the learning of Arabic can be an important part of maintaining Sino-Muslim heritage, while Rumsey (2010) and Bhatt (2023) have shown the importance of religious language in heritage and religious literacies.

More recent work has also looked at the role of cognition in and around religious language (Chilton & Kopytowska, 2018; Richardson et al., 2021), with studies examining how, in particular, metaphor plays a role in understanding in talk about religion (Richardson & Mueller, 2022) or in different metaphorical conceptions of God (Dorst & Klop, 2017), or exploring metaphors in talk about religious belief and practice as it affects experience (Ringrow, 2020b). The research includes analysis of interview settings (Richardson, 2012), moderated discussions (Richardson et al., 2020), online interactions and postings (Pihlaja, 2018; Ringrow, 2020a), and media discourse (Al-Hejin, 2015; Bruce, 2018). This work has begun to focus more explicitly on data from interaction, seeing religious identity and religious language as something which occurs in everyday talk in religious contexts but also in political, social, and educational contexts (Pihlaja, 2021a; Pihlaja & Ringrow, 2023). This research has shown the impact of religious belief and practice on a variety of different contexts where language could be used.

Religious language is, of course, not the only marker of a person's religious beliefs. Indications of religious belief can become evident in a variety of other sites in discourse, including simply how a person physically presents and the way they speak. Moreover, in contexts where people's religious identity is not known or easily deduced from the context or where people of different religions share spaces where others might not necessarily be familiar with the other's beliefs, talk about religious belief is particularly important to the achievement of that belief as part of one's identity. Certainly, non-linguistic cues and semiotic markers are associated with different religious beliefs – a woman wearing a hijab (head covering) in the UK is generally assumed to be Muslim – but identity as a religious believer is confirmed and achieved through discourse. What categories of belief are available and what those categories mean does, however, shift. Different elements of a faith can be more important at different times in discourse, particularly when people of different faiths are interacting; Muslims, for example, must often respond to dominant beliefs in Christianity rather than present their belief on their own terms (Pihlaja, 2021b). Although someone might assume that a woman wearing a hijab is a Muslim and connect that assumption to some understanding of what Muslims generally believe, making any specific judgements about any one individual's experience based on a simple categorical label is problematic.

Rather than focus only on 'religious language', this Element will investigate how religious identity emerges in and through narrative about everyday life. Discourse and conversation analysts, social psychologists, and sociologists have long been interested in the interconnection between storytelling and identity formation. Building upon Labov's (1972) investigations of how identity is shaped through narrative, research has demonstrated that stories appear in natural interaction and are not bound to a specific structure. Instead, they can involve multiple participants who contribute throughout a conversation, oriented towards a conversation's trajectory rather than the structure of a particular story (Jefferson, 1978). Georgakopoulou's (2006, 2007) use of 'small' stories and subsequent investigations into narratives within interactions (Bamberg & Georgakopoulou, 2008; De Fina & Georgakopoulou, 2011) have further underscored the significance of storytelling in everyday communication. Work of conversation analysts like Jefferson (1978) using authentic data has showcased how narratives contribute to the formation of identity. Specific to this research, stories can be used to present religious identities, particularly when those identities are not made obvious by other contextual features.

Research on verbal interaction in superdiverse contexts has shown the effects of these fluid identities on people's language practices (Blommaert & Rampton, 2012). In the study of language in increasingly diverse contexts, *translanguaging* (García & Li, 2014), or the use of different languages, dialects, or modalities, has become more central to questions of how different identities emerge and interest in day-to-day discourse. A project entitled 'Translation and Translanguaging: Investigating Linguistic and Cultural Transformations in Superdiverse Wards in Four UK Cities' (*Translation and Translanguaging (TLANG)*, n.d.), conducted between 2014 and 2018, looked specifically at multilingual interaction in business, education, and recreational contexts, showing how the need to communicate impacted discourse in a wide range of social practices. A key finding from this study was that people used whatever resources were available to them in a given interactive context and that in looking for common ground, people actively tried and found means of communicating around linguistic and cultural barriers. However, within this project, the researchers did not look specifically at religious identity as a variable in these interactions or at interactions about religion between people of different faiths, both key parts of community life in superdiverse contexts. Because religion can be an important part of identity and motivates individual action, understanding the role it plays in discourse in superdiverse contexts has the potential to help researchers better understand how religious identity can affect translanguaging.

While there have been some critiques of 'superdiversity' (Pavlenko, 2018) as a slogan or as being ahistorical and reifying normative assumptions about language (Flores & Lewis, 2016), the term has proven to have staying power in describing, albeit imperfectly, the specific changing contexts of places like Birmingham. Indeed, the interaction among people of different religious identities can also be viewed through the theoretical lens of superdiversity (Becci et al., 2017). Superdiversity has largely been used to describe ethnic and linguistic differences; Burchardt and Becci (2016, p. 6) have described 'religious superdiversity' as both 'religion in the context of superdiversity' and the 'internal diversity of practices, identities and epistemologies' within religious communities. Their research has shown how religious identities are not simply demographic categories of difference as they are often represented in the media, but rather that there are rich internal complexities and differences within religions. They also showed, however, that these complexities can be very difficult to articulate with empirical data, particularly when relying on self-reporting by religious believers about their own beliefs and practices. Burchardt and Becci then argued that close analysis of what people say about their own identity and how they see their identity changing and adapting in superdiverse contexts is needed to understand how religious beliefs and practices are changing in the contemporary world. Religious identity and narrative become increasingly complex where people are regularly in contact with people from different cultures and communities. In such contexts, common-sense understandings of religious categories are challenged by groups of people who might not fit neatly into those categories, with discursive work required to position oneself and one's beliefs.

The relationship between religious and linguistic diversity and social relations has been of interest to many researchers working with, in particular, minority religious groups and immigrant communities. Bredvik (2020) has looked at how linguistic and religious diversity affect the way that people talk about themselves and their faith, particularly how convivial relationships emerge in interaction between people of different faith, ethnic, and linguistic backgrounds. Rosowsky (2008), Gregory and colleagues (2013), and Lytra and colleagues (2016) have also explored multilingualism and its relationship with literacy, both showing the deep relationship that exists between language practice and faith, particularly as it relates to coming to understand oneself in relation to one's community and the rituals and texts that are central to different religious communities. In contexts where English is the dominant language, the relationship between minority languages and religious ritual can grow stronger, particularly if religious contexts are the primary spaces in which minority languages are spoken and maintained. This serves as an additional reinforcing mechanism for the close relationship between different parts of one's identity.

Of course, religious superdiversity has not been universally accepted as a positive thing. Particularly in reporting on Muslim communities, religious identity is frequently portrayed as a problematic marker of difference (Thompson & Pihlaja, 2017). Media coverage of Muslims and other minority religions is consistently negative (Baker et al., 2013; Bruce, 2018) and includes media sensationalism, such as around the so-called Trojan Horse scandal in Birmingham, where Muslims were accused of taking over local school governing boards and promoting and imposing rules based on an understanding of Islamic theology (Clark & Osborne, 2014). These different issues show that although demographic shifts have occurred, historical power structures are maintained and religious belief, ethnicity, and language use can still be sources of discrimination. Moreover, superdiversity may be a useful frame for understanding large metropolitan areas like Birmingham, but this diversity is not necessarily equally distributed throughout the city. Different areas may still be quite monolithic, with segregation occurring for any number of different reasons to do with class, immigration histories, and family connections.

The research thus far reviewed in this section has shown how religious language and religious discourse can be difficult to isolate, with religious identity being integrated in many different elements of an individual's daily experience. The following section describes how these different parts of identity can be explored in discourse.

Methods

This Element is based on research done as a part of an eighteen-month (2021–2) project called 'Language and Religion in the Superdiverse City' (Superdivercity). The project was funded by a UK Arts and Humanities Council (AHRC) leadership fellowship and it was concerned with religious identity as it relates to experiences with people of different faiths. There was an explicit focus on religious organisations that were involved in community activism and organising, building on the findings of the TLANG project and my own previous work looking at how religious diversity was experienced by primary school communities (Pihlaja et al., 2022; Whisker et al., 2020). I was interested in answering the following questions: first, how does religious identity affect the way people interact in superdiverse contexts? Second, how do people perceive their religious identities to be affected by living in superdiverse contexts? And third, how can understandings of thinking and talking about religious identity in superdiverse contexts be used to identify and achieve shared goals among individuals and civil society associations?

The fellowship connected work done in various academic contexts, using linguistic and religious superdiversity, and language and religion, to understand how religious identity, superdiversity, and discourse interact, thereby connecting three key strands of research. Through collecting and analysing data from religious believers in Birmingham, I was interested in addressing three significant academic gaps in our understanding of language, religion, and superdiversity: (1) in language and religion, which has not yet fully investigated the role of language in everyday interaction in superdiverse contexts; (2) in linguistic superdiversity, which has not explicitly focused on how differences in religious belief and practice impact on discourse; and (3) in religious superdiversity, which requires further empirical data to better understand how religious identities develop and shift in superdiverse contexts and the consequences of these shifts on community life.

This Element is the result of that project and presents how religious identity is achieved in stories about lived experience. Through a close analysis of the interview data I collected during the project, the analysis shows how people come to talk about their own identity in light of the larger community context. It focuses on the different elements of identity and experience that come up as people answer questions about who they are and why they view themselves the way they do, ending with some reflections on the consequences of those findings for people that want to better know how to interact with others in their own diverse contexts.

The overarching research methodology for this project was linguistic ethnography and linguistic discourse analysis. Linguistic ethnography is an approach to language as social practice and builds on work in linguistic anthropology and interactional sociolinguistics (Creese, 2008), focusing on how language is used in particular contexts over different timescales. It claims that 'language and social life are mutually shaping, and that close analysis of situated language use can provide both fundamental and distinctive insights into the mechanisms and dynamics of social and cultural production in everyday activity' (Rampton et al., 2012, p. 2). Further, it holds that analysis of language in interaction must 'combine close detail of local action and interaction as embedded in a wider social world' (Creese, 2008, p. 233). Situated discourse analysis investigates not simply what a person says but how they say it. Using situated discourse analysis and longitudinal observation, analysts can provide empirical evidence for how language creates and sustains individual identity and social life.

For this project, where identifying patterns of language and storytelling was the goal, I knew that empirical linguistic data would be necessary, but that understanding and analysing this data would require background knowledge and that ethnographic work – spending time in a place and observing and talking to people without an explicit goal – would provide invaluable information about what people were saying and why. Although I had lived in Birmingham for more than seven years at the beginning of the project, I had, for example, never actually been inside a mosque, despite having friends and colleagues who regularly attended Friday prayers. I planned, in the project, to give myself at least three months of unstructured time to better understand the landscape of the city and meet people where they were, without any expectation of returning to ask people to participate in the project.

I began by approaching the leadership group of Citizens UK, which I had been affiliated with through my university for many years. Citizens UK is a non-partisan national charity that works with civil society organisations to identify and address social and political issues, with chapters all across the country. Birmingham's chapter was founded in the early 2010s, and by the time I became involved in 2016 it had over twenty-five affiliated organisations. Citizens UK includes people of all different faith and ethnic categories and regularly convenes citizens assemblies, including before elections to ask and pressure political leaders and politicians to take the collective concerns of the allied organisations seriously. These organisations include a remarkable mix of people, young and old, from around the city, working together to produce collective action. The leadership group was eager to support the project and use the findings from the project to support dialogue among their organisations.

In a project looking to analyse how people of different religious beliefs understand their own identity in a superdiverse context, where and how to gather data is a challenging question. Because my interest was not necessarily in so-called religious or sacred language, but rather how people talked about their beliefs in day-to-day life, places of religious practice – churches, mosques, gurdwaras – did not seem like the obvious places to meet project participants. Moreover, because of the connection with Citizens UK at the start of the project, and my interest in learning from community organisers and feeding back to them the findings from the project, I began my fieldwork for this project doing one-to-ones with people involved in Citizens UK. One-to-ones are an important part of community-organising work: they are semi-structured conversations where an organiser asks someone about their story and self-interest and looks to build a public relationship with that person, ending with the organiser asking the participant to introduce them to others in their community (Christens, 2010). Building on those conversations and relationships, organisers can then find shared interests and work with people to achieve their own goals.

Here, I encountered my first ethical issue in that, although I had applied for and received ethical approval from my university and had a clear protocol for how I would inform and gain consent from people who formally took part in the research as interview participants, everyone I was encountering was participating in the research even if they weren't sitting for a formal interview. In this case, the principles of community organising were useful in developing an ethical approach to how I was interacting with those around me. For community organisers, there is an important distinction between public and private relationships, and the one-to-one conversations that organisers pursue and take part in are not meant to be places for people to disclose personal struggles, but rather to talk in a public way, sharing information that they are comfortable disclosing to someone they have just met. This principle of engaging with a person's public persona also applied to how people talked about their faith with me: they were presenting their own religious beliefs, but in a way that they would publicly talk about their faith with people who may or may not share those same opinions. I then used these informal conversations to better understand larger community structures rather than seeing them as a place to gather specific information from specific individuals.

The one-to-one conversations often included meeting people where they worked and lived: a walk through a neighbourhood that led to meeting people on their doorstep as they talked about their lives; a meeting in a local mosque with members who had come to pray; a chat with a priest in his office with electric guitars hung on the wall. Throughout the summer of 2021 I met with anyone who would talk with me, wherever they wanted to meet, starting with the leaders from Citizens UK Birmingham and following connections as they developed. I kept fieldnotes from these conversations, recording them as soon after the conversations as I could. In these fieldnotes, I used my memory of the conversations to make notes of themes or non-specific quotes or phrases I remembered that I thought might be important or interesting and which I might want to revisit later. I also included notes about my own feelings and experiences. The following examples are from a conversation with Margaret (pseudonym) on an estate outside of the city that we walked through while talking about her experiences living in the estate and how it had changed over the years.

> We talked about the houses and when they were made: 1972 the estate was established meant to connect with the natural beauty. I thought of MK [Milton Keynes].
> We talked about fitting in and where I was (Harborne) which is where Margaret grew up, but now she feels a part of the estate.
> I said that it would be clear, I thought, that I wasn't from around there, and how I had people stare at me when I jogged through. Margaret said the kids wouldn't see people exercising often.
> We talked about the cost of living and the need for people to survive on £120 a fortnight. The cost of an apartment is not that cheap though, even though everything is in the council.
> We talked about people taking care of their different gardens. Then our own personal families: Margaret has three kids, two of whom are adults and grew up with serious disabilities.

I did not, in these conversations, have a specific agenda about religious belief and experience, and was focused on hearing people talk about what was important to them. Inevitably, however, given the nature of my work and the name of the project, conversations would turn to questions of religious identity and how people saw themselves and others in their neighbourhoods in terms of religious belief. These comments were always, however, oriented towards the interviewer as an outsider, given the diversity of participants.

My own public identity became relevant in these conversations and it was important for me to also establish my boundaries for what I was and was not willing to discuss. I was, at the time of the research, in my late thirties, an immigrant to the UK who first came in 2008 from the US, by way of Japan. I was married to a Japanese woman and we had three young girls, all in their preteens and teens at the time of the research. I am a white cis-gendered, heterosexual man but I, like many of the people I spoke with, am also an immigrant. I have a difficult-to-place Midwestern American accent, something that often prompted discussions about regional accents and attitudes towards different accents. I grew up in a very religious, fundamentalist, Evangelical Christian home in the US, but in my mid-twenties had lost my faith. However, in recent years, I had been attending an Anglican church with my partner, who was a Christian, and had started to take communion again in the church, despite not describing myself as a Christian or believing in Christian theology.

These different complications in my own personal life and history, and how they affected my personal relationships, regularly came up in these informal conversations. Unlike the formal interviews that followed, I often spoke much more in these interactions and shared, when I was comfortable and when I thought it might be advantageous to build rapport, different parts of my own story, of gaining and losing faith, of immigration, and of living and working in Birmingham. The one-to-ones always oriented, in one way or another, to the interests I brought to the conversation and because I initiated the meetings, even though they were more equal in terms of the share of the conversation, they were still generally oriented to my interests as a researcher. I also took part in training for Citizens UK and for academic leadership, as this was an element of the fellowship, and these different courses influenced how I subsequently interacted with participants.

In all, I recorded and kept notes on just over fifty conversations from May 2021 until March 2022. These included negotiated visits to charities within the city, where I met with people and was given tours, but also chance meetings on the bus and visits to places of worship where I didn't know anyone and appeared without any warning, most surprisingly at a charismatic church, where a majority of the congregants were Black British and I was the only white person. There were repeat conversations with some people, particularly those that I worked with through Citizens UK, or people who showed particular interest in the project and with whom I met to get advice about what I was learning. A few of these conversations did result in formal interviews, but more than 90 per cent of the people I met and spoke with during this period of the research did not formally take part in an interview.

Following the period of fieldwork and one-to-one conversations and site visits, I began to approach individuals about taking part in formal interviews for the project. I had my first interview in September 2021 and the last one in April 2022, conducting twenty-four interviews with a total of twenty-five people (see Table 1). Overall, the twenty-five people interviewed for the project came from a variety of different backgrounds, ethnicities, faiths, and ages. The experiences and responses in the full corpus of data represent a vast spectrum of perspectives, but as with any linguistic ethnographic project focused on

Table 1 Participant information.

No.	Pseudonym	Description
1.	Aisha	Young adult woman of Pakistani descent, raised Muslim
2.	Susan	Middle-aged white Methodist woman
3.	Naomi	Middle-aged Jewish woman
4.	Helen	Young adult Black Christian woman, born in the Caribbean
5.	Sophie	Young adult white Anglo-Catholic woman
6.	Charles	Retired white Anglo-Catholic man
7.	Jonathan	Retired white Catholic man, of Irish descent
8.	Esther	Young adult white woman, raised in a Catholic household
9.	Amrit	Middle-aged Sikh woman, of East African Asian descent
10.	Priya	Middle-aged Sikh woman, of Indian descent
11.	Abdul	Middle-aged Muslim man, of Indian descent
12.	Kerry	Young adult white woman, no religious affiliation
13.	Michaela	Young adult Black woman, raised in a Rastafarian household
14.	Margaret	Middle-aged white woman, no religious affiliation
15.	Shabina	Middle-aged Muslim woman, of Bangladeshi descent
16.	Catherine	Young adult white woman, no religious affiliation
17.	Alexandra	Middle-aged white Methodist woman and European immigrant
18.	Omar	Middle-aged Muslim man, of Bangladeshi descent
19.	Hajrah	Middle-aged Muslim woman, of Bangladeshi descent
20.	Nadia	Middle-aged Muslim woman, of East African Asian descent
21.	Allen	Middle-aged white Quaker man
22.	Amy	Middle-aged white Anglican woman
	David	Middle-aged white agnostic man
23.	Richard	Retired white Christian man
24.	Paul	Middle-aged Black Methodist man, immigrant from southern Africa

diversity, producing a representative sample of the religious population is not the goal. Rather, the sample provides *a* set of perspectives on religious diversity in Birmingham, one that will never be fully representative of the city.

The participants agreed to be anonymised as a part of the consent process, and for the purpose of this Element names have been replaced with pseudonyms in all cases. I have also provided descriptions of the participants, relying as much as possible on their descriptions of themselves from the interview while still maintaining their anonymity. I avoided collecting demographic data from the participants before the interview as I was concerned that this might have a priming effect on participants as they might be oriented to categories that I asked them to disclose. Instead, I relied on their own reporting in the interviews and made educated guesses about their age based on the information from the interview (*young adult* for those post-university to age forty, *middle-aged* for those from forty years to retirement, and *retired* for anyone out of working age). Everyone in the study was post-university age, and except for one participant (whom I have labelled *young adult* rather than *middle-aged*) fell clearly into one category.

The participants were given an information sheet prior to the interviews and asked to consent to being recorded. Because Covid-19 remained a significant concern throughout much of the period of data collection, many of the interviews took place over the online video conferencing platform Zoom. The interviewees, however, consented only for their spoken language to be analysed, although Zoom did provide a video as well as audio recording. Participants were told that the conversation would last roughly thirty minutes and all the interviews lasted between twenty-five and thirty-five minutes. Because of the participant information sheet and the informal conversations that led to people participating in the project, the interviews always tended to focus on religious identity and communities, but there was no requirement for participants to be religious themselves. Several of the participants recruited had no religious affiliation, while others expressed that their religious identity was quite passive. At the same time, some of those who participated were active members of religious communities, in some cases serving religious organisations.

The interviews were semi-structured and focused on three main lines of questioning about the history and identity of the participant, the participant's own community, and how the participant saw their own community interacting with other communities. The interviews largely followed these topics and with a few exceptions, the interview schedule was followed around those main topics. No participants ended the interviews early and none subsequently withdrew. The recorded files were then sent to an independent transcription service that provided complete, whole-word transcription, including fillers and vocalisations, which I then checked for accuracy and consistency.

The subsequent analysis in this Element will focus on analysis of the interviews, but the community-organising element of the project continued. In collaboration with some members of the organisation, I produced an infographic which outlined some of the key steps the analysis had highlighted for positive interaction among people of different faiths. Postcards and posters with the infographic on it were produced and distributed among the different member institutions related to Citizens UK and beyond, including places of worship, schools, and other charity organisations within the city. I also held workshops and training sessions with different organisations about how to approach talk about faith in diverse settings and how talk about religious belief can be used in community organising to have effective one-to-ones and encourage people to speak about their own self-interest while developing productive, public relationships with others in their communities.

The aim of the analysis for this Element is to show how the dynamic nature of positioning affects talk about religious identity, so the interview transcripts will be the focus of the analysis. The first step of the analysis was to understand what people talked about in a general way and what themes could be observed across the different transcripts. The fieldwork, site visits, and one-to-ones served as a familiarising process wherein certain themes began to emerge in my mind about how people spoke about their experiences. The fieldnotes, which included my own reflections, provided a genealogy of the impressions I had of each community that informed my approach to the interviews, uncovering potential areas to be investigated further depending on the participant and their community. Common themes in the interviews were identified first by an analysing the transcripts at individual word and phrase levels using Owen's (1984) three criteria: repetition, recurrence, and forcefulness. These different criteria could be applied to a single transcript, for example, looking at the repetition of the category of Catholic being used multiple times to describe a kind of behaviour or action, or could be viewed across transcripts, looking for the use of the word in different transcripts, with the aid of AntConc (Anthony, 2021) software for concordancing. Recurrence could be observed when similar actions or behaviours were described, again either within a single transcript or across transcripts. Finally, forcefulness included times when participants either explicitly stated that something was important or the way they spoke – the volume or prosody – indicated that a point was important. This analysis was also informed by the fieldnotes from site visits and my own tacit knowledge from my time on the project, wherein I gathered, for example, that Indian migration through Africa and the experiences of families coming to England and Birmingham in the 1960s and 70s was a recurring theme in certain immigrant stories.

Having done the initial thematic analysis, I then moved on to consider how categories and positionings emerged in talk. In the previous section, I noted how interest in identity categories and how they emerge in discourse activity has been studied from different perspectives within discourse analytic traditions in psycholinguistics and sociolinguistics. In contrast to cognitive approaches that consider how categories work in the mind, positioning theory (Harré & van Lagenhove, 1998) considers the emergence of positionings within interaction.

This approach is interested in the social action of positionings and how it is context dependent, with different social positionings being taken on by different people in different social situations. These positionings become salient depending on the context (i.e. my position of father is more salient when I am with my children than when I am lecturing) and how they fit into larger structures called 'storylines' (i.e. the social understanding of fatherhood engages with well-established understandings about how fathers should behave) that emerge from and in interaction (De Fina & Georgakopoulou, 2011). Positionings can be explicit in interaction, such as when my daughter calls me 'dad', or implicit in interaction, such as when I am interacting with my line manager and I do what she asks because of our implicit positionings as worker and boss.

Storylines are particularly useful for helping make sense of how positioning relates to larger social structures and 'common sense' or accepted moral reasoning (see Jayyusi, 1984). While positioning is a local, discursive process, people position themselves using resources from their social context. The storyline of 'fatherhood' will emerge differently in different social and cultural contexts, so the positioning as a 'father' will mean different things in different contexts. The expectations about what a person positioned as a 'father' should do and be are both locally constructed in the positioning and globally bound to storylines about 'fatherhood' that are available to the participants in the interaction. By identifying and analysing positionings in discourse, and describing the storylines within which they fit, the analyst can then produce a rich description of both the participants' understanding of themselves and the social world wherein the interaction is occurring.

Understandings of categorisation and positionings are not necessarily oppositional (Deppermann, 2013), but positioning analysis allows for a specific focus on the relationship between the individual positionings that emerge in discourse and their dynamic nature in that discourse. Moreover, they can also reveal relationships in larger structures that can explain how and why positionings emerge when they do. In this research, positioning is also useful because it can occur without explicit mention of categories. Analysis of positioning then provides a context for discussion of important social contexts that may be occurring as the result of the interaction of different contexts, actions, or people. Positioning might, for example, allow for a discussion of how certain identities might become relevant without needing to be explicitly stated. It allows for analysts to orient towards and be informed by potential storylines about belief embedded in the cultural context that might be present beyond a particular conversation or discourse event and take into account, in the case of this project, the other ways of speaking about recurring events, having been identified in the initial thematic analysis.

My own adaptation of positioning analysis systematises the process of identifying positions and storylines, allowing for them to be identified at different points in the discourse, with the goal of seeing how they change over time. The process of segmenting and identifying positioning in discourse activity followed Pihlaja (2021b, p. 36):

1. Transcribe discourse event.
2. Segment discourse event (following Cameron, 2010).
3. Identify all explicit positionings in each segment.
4. Consider potential implicit positionings, including of the speaker and audience, searching for further evidence of these positionings elsewhere in the event.
5. Identify the explicit storyline or implicit storyline the positionings constitute.
6. For each positioning, describe its trajectory in the discourse event.
7. Compare positionings of speakers within the discourse event and across discourse events.

These positionings were analysed in their first instance in the interviews, and then traced through the duration of the interview to see how certain themes develop over the course of the discourse activity and what these instances might reveal about larger conceptions of religious identities and how particular faiths are viewed within a given context. The method creates a more specific process of looking for positionings in discourse and introduces the discourse dynamics notion of *trajectories* (Cameron, 2015) to the analysis of positioning, suggesting that positionings, like any other element of discourse, are on an evolving path, emerging and changing and adapting over the course of the discourse activity.

The method reveals that within a discourse event, each positioning is not isolated in a static moment but is a dynamic part of a larger structure. Therefore, segmenting the discourse event allows for the analyst to first see the macro development of the interaction and then in turn understand how each positioning is emerging at different levels of the discourse event: a single intonation unit, within an utterance, within a conversation turn, within a topic, or within a whole interaction. Next, identifying explicit positionings is often the most straightforward step because they are often voiced as categories, such as a participant saying of themselves, 'As a Sikh'. These can also be negations of categories, like a participant saying 'I'm not a Christian', wherein the meaning of 'Christian' must be understood from what has come before and after that statement and what is meant by it in a specific interaction. Each positioning operates within a storyline of actions and contexts revealing how each person understands themselves and others. From this point, the analyst can then consider where implicit positionings might be occurring. For example, in the dataset a Black Christian man, who is not British, refers to another as a 'white, British Christian'. Although he never explicitly says that he is a 'Black, non-British Christian man', that position is made clear in the reference to others.

Building on that information and the thematic analysis, the analyst can then begin to identify potential storylines that might be present in the discourse, considering not just what an individual is saying about themselves in the world but also what others have said and how they compare with one another. In this project as well, I could recognise larger structures from the one-to-ones and site visits I did during the fieldwork stage, wherein I didn't record the specific things that people said but recalled broadly the trajectories of their stories. This allowed me to consider how the same positionings were accomplished by different people of the same religious belief or how the same positionings were accomplished by people of different religious beliefs, and so on. The analysis could then consider each different positioning with a larger context of discourse activity, not to make a claim about the interpretation of a particular statement but to better understand how someone's positioning compared with other participants' positionings.

To better understand how positionings connected to storylines, I employed the concept of *abstraction* (see Pihlaja, 2023). Within cognitive linguistics, *abstraction* refers 'to the process that … allows us to form and store … semantic information gleaned across our experiences', and which enables humans to 'discern what various objects and events have in common, and group them together into concepts' (Yee, 2019, p. 1257). The emergence of storylines and the salience of positionings within them must require some connection between concrete lived experience and thinking about those experiences in abstract ways that allow for moral judgements, but it became clear in the data that abstraction did not simply have two levels, but that people might speak at different levels of abstraction, for example, speaking about an event occurring on a specific street, or in a specific neighbourhood, or in Birmingham as whole, or in the UK, with each level of higher abstraction having more consequences for the generalisability of a claim.

I began by attempting to develop a coding structure for abstraction using the online coding tool EMargin (https://emargin.bcu.ac.uk/) and trying to identify different levels of abstraction and where they were occurring in the discourse. I developed a coding structure and worked with an MA student on placement with the project for several months, Celine Quinn, to determine the replicability of a process of marking levels of abstraction. Celine undertook her own interviews related to religious diversity, in addition to helping to develop the coding procedure. After working unsuccessfully to code a whole utterance by level of abstraction, I instead chose to analyse utterances within stories by word, looking at how abstraction occurred in actors, actions, places, and times (Pihlaja, 2023), showing that, for example, when an individual was abstracted to a particular category and described in a story as taking an action, it revealed how storylines about categories of people developed. For example, in a story about the racist actions of a particular group of people, a participant commented, 'A racist person would never sort of differentiate whether you're Muslim, Hindu, Sikh', suggesting that the actions of people in the group followed a prototypical way of acting for racists (see the 'Racism and Tension' section for further analysis of this extract). That way of talking about how a particular group of people act and what is typical of them is a good example of a storyline emerging from a particular story. The story is both evidence of and evidence for a way of understanding the world.

Using these principles, the following analysis considers how positionings can be traced within each interview and what these positionings might reveal about larger conceptions of religious identities and how particular faiths are viewed. The goal of the analysis is to show the different ways religious identity emerged from the stories of experience and how participants' experience and understanding of those stories shaped how they viewed the world. The extracts analysed over the next three sections have been chosen for their exemplar quality and to represent as many of the participants as possible. Following the overarching themes from the interviews, the sections will cover how people come to understand themselves (Self-Identity and Construction), how they understand and experience the world around them (Building Community), and how living in a diverse context shapes their day-to-day lives (Living Superdiversity).

Self-Identity and Construction

Previous research (reviewed in the first section) has shown that religious identity is a complex site of the intersection of personal histories and experiences. These experiences can be shared among the same community, for example, when communities are composed of people who have immigrated around the same time, from the same place, and have shared beliefs. Individual and shared experiences are not necessarily discrete and distinct categories and participants often talked about their experiences in relation to an understanding of what others have experienced. On the other hand, participants often highlighted that particular experiences were unique to their own lives, even when evidence from other interviews and site visits suggested that others had similar experiences. This section discusses themes related to personal identity construction as they emerged in the data, with a specific focus on how these individual stories related to storylines about religious belief and practice and how they contributed to a participant's positioning of themselves.

Personal History

In the interviews, the first question was oriented towards eliciting the participant's positioning of themselves as it related to their personal history and family. The question was worded as something like, 'If you could start by telling me a little bit about your background, erm so where did you grow up, erm and erm erm where you originally come from . . . that, the area, that sort of thing' (interview with Esther) and often reflected a shared nervousness at the start of the interview and my own attempt to simply start the conversation. Sometimes, depending on the participant and my familiarity with their position (if, for example, they were a former Catholic priest), I did on occasion prime a focus on faith in my first question (i.e. 'Tell me about your experiences growing up Catholic'). The participants chose to respond to this question in different ways, going back in history in different scales. Several examples include:

(1) I grew up, I was born in Nottingham. Erm I grew up in a family that were ah Baptists so erm probably until I was about eleven. Went to Sunday school, was involved very much in the church as a child. Erm and I do remember about the age of seven, erm having a real sense of God's presence and really challenging my family on questions of faith at that age. (Susan)

(2) So in terms of my background, my heritage, I'm Bangladeshi. So came to, to the UK in Birmingham in 1982 when I was four years old, erm so erm came here to join my dad, who was here from 1961. Erm so I came with my mum and my three older siblings, and-and since then, erm for the last erm thirty-eight, thirty-nine years, have more or less lived in Birmingham. (Shabina)

(3) Yes, so, I was raised in [neighbouring area in Birmingham] erm by my parents who were Rastas, who are Rastas still. Erm yeah, we grew up in a very . Black area. So, [neighbouring area in Birmingham] is predominantly Black, erm and then after that, I would probably erm say, Asians, with erm a very small minority of erm of white-white people. (Michaela)

The question of 'Where are you from' and the invitation to 'tell me a little about yourself' led people to position themselves first in terms of physical location, with different features of (1) history of religious experience, (2) family history in the place, and (3) racial and ethnic identity. In all three of these interviews, this starting point for the participant proved important for the trajectory of the interview, as in each case here and in the all of the interviews, participants responded to the prompt in slightly different ways that had consequences for how they eventually spoke about themselves or their families going forward. Where participants focused on place in the initial response, place became a significant theme in the first parts of the interview. For those who first spoke about family, the theme of the family was recurring in the initial talk about their religious identity.

For all the participants, the relationship of who they are and where they came from played some part in how they positioned themselves, either in opposition to how they were raised or in explaining who they were. For participants from religious groups that have been historically in the minority in the country, how their family related to the community and were seen by others also played a significant role in positioning themselves as, for example, being the only Muslim in a non-Muslim education setting (Aisha) or a Black Rastafarian family in a context with many Christians (Michaela). These stories highlighted how a participant's religious identity as a child corresponded to their family's identity, often being a minority in terms of ethnicity as well, with consequences for how they viewed themselves where they grew up.

Religious histories within family life were closely tied to stories of their own family's immigration to the country and positioning within storylines of their own community's experience of coming to the UK.

(4) So, yeah, so, my, my, uh, grandfather on my father's side had come to, um, England from India . . . In the sixties. And he'd sort of . . . Um, well, bought a house, worked and lived with . . . A bit like how the Polish male workers . . . When they first came to this country were like . . . So they'd all live in one big house . . . And they'd rent rooms to other people from his village . . . Who he, he managed to get jobs for. So, he sort of started a community up like that, really. Then, after he, he . . . He then went back to India, and had a, bought a house, so his sons could come and live there. So, that's how the, the, kind of, the family came over, really. (Priya)

(5) Yeah, so I'm erm born in Bangladesh, erm 1978 erm my dad erm was a college lecturer and an imam part-time [unclear]. So he moved erm a week after I was born to the UK to uh be an imam somewhere in [small town] in the north [of England]. Erm so I uh with my erm sisters joined my dad as a erm immigrant in uh 1984 in the UK erm then he changed his job, moved around and have been living here in Birmingham since 1985 erm consequently two weeks before what's known as the Handsworth Riots. (Omar)

(6) So, the core parish was a rather well-established English Catholic
community, but with then, a lot of Irish immigrants who joined, and a few
Polish and a few Italian and so on. But mainly, Irish then. And then
gradually over the years . . . So when my father came, you know, he was a,
sort of, outsider really, uh, or on the edge of the community. (Jonathan)

Immigration played a role in how many positioned themselves. In the first
example, Priya talks about how her grandfather came to England from India and
describes how the family was established, also providing an account, through
analogy to Polish workers, of big families living together in one home. There is
no mention of Sikhism or her own family's Sikh identity, but within this story of
her family's immigration, she notes that her grandfather 'started a community
up'. In Omar's story of his family coming to England, there is a more explicit
place for religion because of his father's role as an imam, but his subsequent
description of his father and the life of the family positions them in a storyline of
struggles, where his father has difficulty finding work and speaking English but
serves as a community leader. Jonathan's story of family immigration relates the
experience of his father as an Irish Catholic coming to England and his experiences as an outsider even within the institution of the Catholic Church, which in
Birmingham has been an important community institution for Irish immigrants.
In the story of Jonathan's father, he is positioned as an outsider, both in his
religious identity and in his experiences within religion.

For the Sikh and Muslim participants in the study, all of them included a story
of how their families or they themselves came to England, and the location of
communities of faiths, in particular the location of mosques and gurdwaras,
served as an important element in how communities emerged. In my fieldwork,
I visited a Filipino pastor living and serving a church of predominately Filipino
immigrants in a deprived estate, with the same storyline of immigration recurring in his talk: mothers and fathers coming over for work and sending for their
families later; settling in places that were known to them, often on one or two
streets in a community; and establishing a community around a place of
worship, with national, ethnic, and religious identities coming together.

In contrast to the stories of immigration, wherein people positioned themselves
and their faiths as part of an ethnic and national identity, several participants told
stories of conversion to their faith.

(7) Before I was a Christian I would have identified as a militant atheist and um,
yeah, there was, there was definitely a time I would have identified as an
atheist, militant atheist. And quite an unpleasant person. I know one's not
necessarily proud to reveal that but none the less I was bad egg um, about
that. And I would be quite open about that when I went to confirmation

classes in my thirties. I was quite open about the fact um, that I was um, quite an unpleasant character in terms of religious discourse really. But as I say, I do know a lot of people who are atheist or agnostic or non-practising, who have various faith upbringings who are by no means a rotten egg but that was just how I was. (Amy)

(8) Um, [my parents] didn't take us to church, but when I was about five, I remember suddenly realising that God was real. And, um, being completely obsessed with school, because I loved school, and I heard that you could [go] on a Sunday. So, I asked to go to Sunday School. Um, so, my dad would drop us off and then leave us there and pick us up after church, my brother and I. (Sophie)

In Amy's story about her faith, she contrasts her identity as a 'militant atheist' with her identity as a Christian, drawing a clear distinction between who she was before she was a Christian with who she became afterwards. She positions her previous self as 'militant' and as 'a rotten egg' before converting, while clarifying that this was specific to her own experience and that she didn't view other atheists or agnostics in a negative way. Sophie's story of coming to faith doesn't include the contrast with a previous life, but rather with her own parents whom she positions as not having particular religious beliefs themselves. Instead, she independently realised that 'God was real' and started attending church and becoming involved, saying after recounting her involvement in various other activities as a teenager: 'So, I had a, a very strong faith.'

Both stories and how they position the teller do important work for not only explaining an individual's own religious beliefs but also positioning themselves as agents in their own story. The contrasts that emerge, either with a previous life or with one's own family, position them as having personal ownership of their faith and a confidence in that positioning. That positioning, and the confidence shown in it, has consequences for how they then position themselves throughout the interaction, as having chosen their own belief and, in both cases, dealing with doubt in different ways. Even as Sophie later recounts a shifting in her faith from Evangelical Christianity to Anglo-Catholicism, she says, when prompted to contrast her two positions: 'Well, I suppose before contrasting, I would say that the similarities is the very strong faith in what we believe.' This positioning reinforces a consistency in the trajectory of her story about herself, as a confident, committed person of faith.

In all these cases, regardless of how they viewed their experiences in the past and growing up, participants, in reflecting on their own identity, made use of stories of experience from the past to provide context for how they currently viewed themselves. Their own positioning was a part of a life story, which they recounted in a way that provided a rationale for how they developed. Religious identity was something that emerged from their recounting of life experience and with rare exception was not articulated as a clear set of beliefs. At the same time, the individual instantiations of these stories had shared characteristics with other stories and related to ways of talking and thinking about particular groups of people who have been historically minorities in England. Positioning themselves in relation to a religious identity for all the participants was always related to other elements of identity and personal history.

Markers of Religious Identity

Across the interviews, a participant's religious position often became clear, not usually through an explicit claim to a named religious identity or category, but rather through reference to a place, role, or family member. For example, Naomi first mentions Jewishness in her interview, saying, 'Um, my mum was Jewish. So, she was Jewish but not particularly practising' and Charles introduces himself saying, 'Well, my, my name is Charles. I'm a churchwarden, um, uh, here and I've been attending this church since the early 1980s.' There were also references to faith communities, like when Amrit says, 'Where we were in West London, we were very close to, um, one of the first, uh, Sikh gurdwaras, so, places of worship.' In all of these instances, the participant's religious identity became clear without them explicitly saying they were a member of a particular religious faith.

Aisha, who earlier in the interview identifies as a Muslim in a Catholic school, talks about interactions with others from different faiths, saying, 'Like, I would never introduce myself being, like, oh, I'm, I'm a, I'm Muslim.' She shares this while talking about respecting the beliefs of others and the importance of her religious identity in those contexts and her comment suggests that she sees her religious identity as less relevant in some settings: 'I don't think it's that important.' This feeling is not expressed in precisely the same way by others but does show how positioning oneself in terms of religious belief can and does change depending on the context.

An apparent reticence to identify using a categorical label may relate in some cases to physical appearance. For example, a woman wearing a hijab or vicar's 'dog collar' has little need to claim a religious category. In other cases, face-saving cultural norms (that is, in British culture it may be impolite to explicitly state a religious belief) might have also explained this. Regardless of the reason, the avoidance of categorical labels when positioning oneself appeared to be a way to avoid misunderstanding or a negative judgement that might come from stereotypes about one's community. By self-positioning in a potentially more agreeable way, for example, as a person who accepts others' beliefs and happens to be Muslim, Aisha may be anticipating a positioning of herself in a storyline about Muslims that she wishes to pre-empt.

This self-awareness about how one might be perceived by others because of one's physical appearance was discussed by several participants:

(9) And so, obviously a turban is, uh, kind of very easy and a prime example because, you know, obviously a turban would be associated with, I-I-I-I suppose, you know, uh, uh, a little bit of, um . . . How do you say? Perhaps exotic . . . [Laughing] kind of thing. Kind of exotic dress, or, you know . . . Whatever people thought from the East . . . Or from South Asia, um, uh, and you know, for Sikhs obviously the, the turban is very much about their, you know, connects with, uh, the mind and your value set, [laughs], and, um, uh, you know, this idea of, um, uh, uh, leadership and responsibility. You know, kind of, uh, governing your mind . . . (Amrit)

(10) And then, I think a lot of my family, the women wear a hijab. And I actually wore a hijab for a while as well, and when I did wear one, then people obviously immediately know that you're Muslim. I don't think they treat you any differently, necessarily, but I feel like, when you wear a hijab, you're, you're like representing the entire Muslim population essentially, and there's a lot of pressure. (Aisha)

(11) When I have meetings outside or I'm going somewhere, I am cautious. You know, I'll probably get that look when I'm wearing my hijab. And I will get that look. You, you do have that feeling sometimes. And you're always cautious. (Hajrah)

The contrast between other and self-positioning is explicit in Amrit's discussion of the turban, the perceptions of which she struggles to articulate, coming to 'exotic'. She then contrasts this with the religious and spiritual meaning of the turban to indicate commitment to ideals and the 'mind and value set' and 'governing your mind'. Aisha describes her experience of wearing the hijab, and although she notes that she didn't feel like people treated her differently, she did feel a responsibility to represent Islam and the Muslim community, saying 'there's a lot of pressure' without making explicit what the cause of that pressure is, whether it is internal to her, from the Muslim community, or from outsiders. Finally, Hajrah says she is aware that the wearing of the hijab results in her getting 'that look' or having 'that feeling', which she doesn't further elaborate on, but suggests it is part of a negative positioning of her and one that leads her to be 'more cautious'.

Appearance could go beyond how people dressed specifically and come to include racial and ethnic markers as well.

(12) What I've noticed that, personally, I've-I've noticed that there is always an assumption that this man is from [African country], this man from Africa is Black, uh he must be totally against same-sex marriage. That might be true, but it is an assumption, uh that is not based on uh any understanding of me. (Paul)

(13) You can feel very strongly Jewish without necessarily being religious. And if we mean by religious, fervently believing, going to synagogue, following the rules, whatever those rules may be, um, you know, I'm not, not so good at that bit of it always. (Naomi)

These comments reflect the relationships that can occur between ethnicity and religious identity, both from an internal and external perspective. For Paul, being perceived as a Black man from Africa, he feels positioned by others to hold particular views, something he challenges here and elsewhere in the interview, suggesting that there is a misunderstanding among, in particular, white, British Christians about what Black Christians believe and why. Naomi's comment reflects a tension within some Jewish people about the relationship between being 'religious' and 'feeling' Jewish, two things that she suggests are not necessarily related, giving different examples in the interview of her family members who engage with 'Jewishness' in different ways and see it as an ethnic, religious, and political position, depending on who they are and where they are.

Like the hijab or turban, ethnic identities and how they are perceived to be indications of religious belief had consequences for how participants felt pressure to position themselves in particular ways. These could be negative in the case of racism directed towards them (which I will discuss in more depth in the 'Living Superdiversity' section), but in the examples from Amrit and Aisha, the concern isn't that the turban or hijab will lead to negative judgements, but that they will be misunderstood and they will be positioned in storylines that include misunderstanding of that dress and could lead to, in Aisha's case at least, a reticence to wearing the hijab because of how it might result in her being viewed in a particular and limited way.

On the other hand, Naomi describes a different experience, in choosing to make her own identity evident to those she meets:

(14) It's not . . . I don't know. I don't, on the whole, particularly experience antisemitism. I mean, I've started, after a long time of not doing so, I started wearing a-a Star of David. Partly just to stop passing, um, and-and to be a bit more visible. (Naomi)

Naomi's choice to wear the Star of David is not positioned exclusively as an act of religious commitment or practice but a way of identifying herself to others as Jewish, and explicitly in response to antisemitism, which she describes as not something that she generally experiences but something that she is aware to be occurring, noting that when violence has occurred, the victims have been wearing a kippah, or head covering. By choosing to wear the Star of David, she explains it as a way to stop 'passing', suggesting that she doesn't perceive others as positioning her as a Jewish woman. By wearing a Star of David, she both positions herself as a member of the community and in solidarity with that community.

All of these cases suggest that when a person's religious belief is made evident in their appearance, there is a perception that others will understand the clothing or symbol in a way that may not comport with how the individual wearing the symbol or clothing understands it themselves. The positioning makes clear that a tension is present between how a person views themselves and how others might view them. Given the nature of the questions for the interviews, the participants tended to talk about how this clothing set them apart from others, or made them more visible, but it is also implicitly a marker of shared identity among people wearing the same clothing. Hajrah alludes to this after discussing the potential negative feelings she gets from others, by then talking about the violence done to other women wearing a hijab.

Other less obvious elements came up in discussing markers of religious identity:

(15) I think there is that element of, uh, um, [the gurdwara] connects you to, uh, uh, your Sikh heritage. One, in a cultural sense, because a lot of that heritage is obviously preserved through, you know, music, food, language, all those kind of, uh, expressions of a culture. But I think probably I'm thinking about, um, individuals in my family or Sikhs I've crossed paths with. (Amrit)

Amrit's description of life in and around the gurdwara includes different parts of cultural life that is connected to religion, as the centre of local cultural life was the gurdwara. The religious setting is positioned as a key location for the immigrants and their children, and, in Amrit's case, her own children, to connect to their heritage through the Sikh life that is facilitated by the gurdwara as a local meeting place. Amrit goes on to say that the language also serves as a way of connecting people of different religious backgrounds from the same place in India, showing that shared culture and identity can include people of different faith backgrounds when sharing in the immigrant experience.

What makes someone a member of a particular religious group is both something that emerges through their positioning of their own personal history and how they tell the story of their religious identity, but also is presented in how they position themselves with the way they dress and the symbols they choose to wear, and how their dress, symbols, and ethnic identity influence how others position them. The making of religious identity in the daily lived experience is an interaction among these different components, with the participants themselves seeing meaning in how they are treated by others and attempting to make choices in their own self-positioning that can foreground that identity, as in Naomi's Star of David, background that identity, as in Aisha's choice to not wear a hijab, or accept it as something that they can't avoid, as in Paul's identity as a Black man in a Christian context.

Complications in Religious Identity

Individual histories and personal stories about family belief were a theme in many participant responses when addressing religious identities that weren't straightforward or included some loss or rejection of their previous religious belief, which compared to stories of conversion did not necessarily include a positioning of themselves as an agent making a choice.

(16) Erm so, I was raised Catholic, erm because my mum's Catholic. erm my dad wasn't really religious. And so it was like regular kind of churchgoing and things, erm and all of that, until I was probably in my mid-teens. Then sort of stopped going to church as much, and then I just like, and then I feel like now I'm just sort of at the point I'm like, I don't really know where I'm at. Like, I'm definitely not, a practising Catholic anymore, and I feel like I've, you've gone ... I'm just like, I don't know. (Esther)

(17) So, looking back, yes, I would say that Rasta, or being raised as a Rasta was probably my biggest influence, but I understand that growing up in the area that I grew up in, there was a lot of other Rasta families as well. A lot of other Black families that were into, what we would call Black Consciousness, erm stuff like that. You know African and Pan-Africanism, African Liberation, things like that. (Michaela)

In these two quotes, both Esther and Michaela highlight how their own religious identity is influenced by how they grew up. In Esther's response, there is a clear delineation between herself and her upbringing, saying that she doesn't know what she is anymore, but that she now rejects the category of Catholic for herself. Michaela's response is less clear, in that she indicates that 'Rasta' was her biggest influence, and listing it among a series of other movements that are related to ethnic and political identities rather than religious ones. Rastafarianism, here and throughout her talk, is closely related to the political position her father took and how she was raised to be politically active and engaged in Black liberation.

In both Michaela and Esther's subsequent talk about themselves, how they were raised, and the religious element of that upbringing, plays an important part in how they talk about their own value system and how they engage in the world. Esther goes on to discuss how she remains connected to her Catholic identity despite no longer having that belief, saying that she continues to recognise her connection to Catholicism in day-to-day life and feeling a connection with Catholics, both former and practising, because they 'share the same language'. Michaela, on the other hand, doesn't ever explicitly say what her position is on Rastafarianism, but instead talks about cutting off her dreadlocks on two occasions, one recently. These positionings, both explicitly and implicitly, reveal how upbringing and previous religious beliefs are significant in how religious identities are engaged in discourse activity and how the reticence to use a category of belief does not necessarily indicate a rejection of that belief. For Esther, although she is explicitly and decidedly 'not a practising Catholic', Catholicism is still an important part of how she positions herself.

Although the nature of the project attracted religious believers for whom religion was a positive experience, not all experiences with religious identity were described in this way.

(18) I-I have some very complicated feelings around that period of my life [when I was very religious] because it ended quite badly, I guess, um, which again I can absolutely go into, but I think the [sighs], the, kind of, the emotion that's driven with those type of churches, you know, the songs are very passionate, like, it brings up a lot of feelings. Um, like, I have memories of going on weeklong, ah, residential activities in, like, massive, super churches, and, like, sobbing because [laughs], because . . . I know now music is really emotive, right, it can do anything to you. And at the time, I thought that was . . . I thought that was God working within me. Um, but now I look back and I see it more as manipulation, so it's quite complicated [laughs]. (Catherine)

Here, Catherine recounts her experiences within Evangelical Christianity, having spoken at length about her involvement in a church and before going on to talk about the circumstances of how things 'ended quite badly'. She positions herself first as a believer, very engaged in the work of the church and committed to the church's ministry, and contrasts how she felt about something at the time ('I thought that was God working within me') with her feelings now ('I see it more as manipulation'). The positioning of her current self to when she was a person of faith maps on to a story of trauma, wherein her current positioning affects how she positions her past self, with the awareness that her past self-positioning would have been different. Catherine does not, in this extract or in the transcript, label the process she has undergone, but the reflection on her past and the positioning of herself as having changed her views occurs in a storyline of manipulation rather than agency, with her experience of religious life being presented in a negative way. By telling the story of her religious experience, her current positioning is explained and shows that she has come to the position in a logical and understandable way. Like the stories of conversion, immigration, and upbringing, the positioning of herself with the story of lived experience provides an explanation for her positioning as a part of a trajectory, an ongoing story that is meaningful to her.

For two of the participants, a lack of religious belief was unproblematic and didn't obviously relate to previous trauma.

(19) So I did a theology degree and I've always . . . I've always found learning and understanding about different religions really interesting. I've never felt particularly drawn to one particular faith path. Um, yeah, I wouldn't define myself in terms of one particular religious tradition, but I suppose I've always been interested in spirituality in-in general, um, yeah. (Kerry)

(20) Um, my dad's side is Catholic, there was religion within the family, but my dad didn't pursue it. Um, I used to stay with my dad's sister, my auntie, quite a lot and we'd go to, um, church every Sunday morning when I stopped . . . (Margaret)

In Kerry's response to a prompting about her own religious identity, she connects it to learning in university and positions herself as not being 'drawn to one particular faith path'. Unlike the stories seen elsewhere in this section, she doesn't position herself within a religious background or a family tradition which she either affirms or rejects. For Margaret, she does indicate that she had some relationship with religion in the past, but then simply says that she 'stopped' and has nothing additional to add. In both cases, when I prompted for more information about religious identity, the participants had nothing more to say.

These responses are unique in the dataset but only because the participant selection favoured people with religious beliefs and there was no additional scope to discuss religious identity in non-religious individuals, although this is also a growing demographic in the UK and in Birmingham, with 24 per cent of people responding as having no religion in the 2021 census (Office for National Statistics, 2022). The interaction between people of religious faith and people of no declared religious faith is likely to continue to grow as an important area of interreligious dialogue. At the same time, given the relationship between religious identity and culture seen throughout the whole of this section, separating religion from other parts of one's identity may prove to be more difficult for some people than others. And while for people like Kerry who, having a lack of background in any particular religious faith, see them all equally and are not drawn to one in particular, for people born into immigrant communities wherein religious identity is a part of how their parents and grandparents position themselves, and how they are positioned in media narratives about them, simply setting aside that identity might be more difficult.

Within religious identities, participants positioned themselves in different ways and several participants distanced themselves from elements of their faith tradition to which they positioned themselves as being opposed. Richard, a retired scientist and Christian, says:

(21) Uh, the other thing in my intellectual stroke, ah, spiritual development is the interaction between what I know as a physicist and, and what I believe as, uh, as a Christian. And so, for instance, um, I am perfectly prepared to read the bible and say I accept all kinds of biblical criticism but am trying to understand what really was going on. So, um, for instance if-if I'm in a church where a creed is being said I will be quiet during the bit 'born of virgin Mary'. (Richard)

This extract presents a relatively rare moment in the dataset where a person discusses what they personally 'believe' in an explicit way, but in this case Richard is distancing himself from a part of Christian theology that he otherwise believes. He does this particularly as it relates to a creed, a statement of faith that Christians in many traditions would recite together during a service or Mass as a statement of shared belief. Richard here positions himself as a 'physicist' in addition to a 'Christian' and as a result says that he is 'quiet' when the creed affirms that Jesus was 'born of the virgin Mary', suggesting that he does not share this belief because it doesn't comport with what he understands about the world as a physicist. Within this story, however, Richard first reasserts his own positioning as a Christian, suggesting that being a Christian for him does not require complete agreement with all parts of Christian theology.

Richard's discussion of a particular belief is rare in the whole of the dataset, with few people positioning 'belief' as a core part of their own religious identity. This certainly could be the result of the interview context wherein the participants were talking about their experiences of living in Birmingham rather than being explicitly asked about what they believed. Whether that was the case, the interview data does show that people can effectively talk about their religious identity without focusing on religious faith or belief, and suggests that while precise articulation of one's own belief may be important in some particular religious communities, for many people it isn't a necessary part of talking about religious identity.

Finally, among several of the participants, a reticence to discuss labels and identify faith categories could also be observed. Here, Shabina responds to a question about whether cultural influence is important in how Islam is understood in her community and Michaela talks about her own view of God.

(22) Absolutely, yes. Yeah sometimes we take those culture, people interchange between culture and religion, which for me is something so different, you know because I could be a Muslim from an Arab background, to Pakistani, to you know white, to African, you know and there's, there are five, six continents. And we've got so many different sorts of cultural backgrounds and understandings. So you can't label that barrier as a Muslim barrier, you have to sort of unpick it and realise that it actually you know it could be you know because of where they're from originally, you know something to do with their heritage. (Shabina)

(23) The-the religious aspect in regards to that, no I don't-I don't see it that way. I don't see, I see these things as labels. So, you could call Him, Allah. You can call Him, God. You can call Him, And it's just a different name for the same energy. So, you get me, I don't feel the need to get involved in, you know what I mean, back and forths about, you know what I mean, this future and what this . . . Okay, that's what it means to you, brilliant. And what are you going to birth out of that? Is it beautiful? Wonderful. Do you get what I mean, what are you going to birth out the way that you see? Is it beautiful? Wonderful. (Michaela)

In Shabina's talk about the role of 'culture' and religion, she draws attention to the vastly different perspectives people who are categorised as 'Muslim' hold, highlighting the different countries that people of the Muslim faith come from in her community. She then uses this to position issues, which she metaphorises as 'barriers', that are positioned as ones relating to 'religion' as actually 'cultural' differences. Michaela expresses a positioning of all faiths as the same by speaking of God in various forms as being essentially 'the same energy' and saying that 'he' can be called by many different names, provided that the result of the belief is something 'beautiful'.

Shabina's positioning of 'barriers' as cultural ones counters an implicit storyline of a conflict between British and Islamic values, which was a recurring theme in our interview. The positioning of 'barriers' is then not only a simple explanation for why any individual problem might occur, but a way of thinking about the role of religion and how and why conflicts that appear to be based in religious belief or identity emerge. The storyline provides a heuristic for understanding conflict and for explaining to people outside of the community how they may be misunderstanding 'Muslims' and, indeed, so-called Western cultures. Michaela's articulation of a positive acceptance of all religious perspectives also includes an important storyline, that all good and beautiful things come from the same energy, and also implies a counter-storyline that anything which is not beautiful cannot come from that same energy. This too can serve as a heuristic for judging whether something is from God.

Conclusion

Throughout this section, the role of personal history and lived experience of oneself and one's community in understanding one's own religious identity is clearly evident. For all the participants, self-positioning within a religious context involved not only accounting for themselves and what they believed, but describing how interactions with others, their families, and their own personal histories led to those positions. These self-positionings and the stories from which they emerged are both unique and individual and common among particular types of people, providing evidence that ways of talking about one's belief reflect culturally relevant storylines, ones that can be observed across a range of different participants. The absence of extended discussion of belief and spiritual experience in the interviews in participants' positioning of their own religious identity challenges a notion that religious identity is primarily about religious belief. Certainly, different questions and different participants could have elicited different responses, but the discourse shows how effectively religious identity can be spoken about without a focus on belief.

Building Community

The Element so far has shown how religious identity is never achieved in a vacuum. Religious belief and practice, as we've seen, are deeply embedded in social relationships, with religious institutions playing central roles in the lives of religious people from a variety of different backgrounds. Understanding who someone is and how they understand their religious identity will always involve understanding how they view themselves in a larger community of religious believers, either in how they see themselves as similar to or different from those around them. Having looked at how participants understood their own religious beliefs in light of their experiences, and their family and personal histories, in this section I will turn to how individuals saw themselves in their own religious communities and the larger communities in which they lived in the city, which included people of different and no religious faith. I'll look first at how those communities are constructed and maintained, then how they are perceived to be changing, and finally how people understand service in this superdiverse context.

Making Community

Throughout the interviews, participants were almost always eager to talk about place: about the city they lived in and the physical spaces that were home to the religious communities of which they were a part. In the previous section, I discussed how storylines about immigration were important for many in understanding their religious and cultural identity. Throughout the stories about immigration, the centrality of places of worship for community life, was a common theme:

(1) So, my mosque was everything, even now. I'd go to my mosque . . . It's like a little village, you know. You go for mediation, you go for . . . If you want anything, the nursery is there, seniors are there. From, like, you know, from cradling to grave, so I get everything from my mosque. (Nadia)

(2) Um, where we were in West London, we were very close to, um, one of the first, uh, Sikh gurdwaras, so, places of worship . . . So, quite a, a historic gurdwara in that case, and so it was quite close to us, so that was, uh, um, uh, weekend visits to the gurdwara. So, linked to the gurdwara community. I did also have, um, I suppose quite a rich extended family life. So, um, aunts, um, uncles, and I was quite aware that they had been, kind of, part of a a- earlier generation of, uh, students abroad. So, maybe studied in Europe or Scotland, and so, I-I, in a way they were, like, my kind of [laughing] role models for going out in the world. But, um, uh, also, uh, you know, taking part of your identity with you wherever you go. So, uh, parents, uncles, aunt and aunts and both sets of grandparents, so, uh, I kind of, uh, I suppose, uh, [laughing] I had the village and the city kind of superimposed on each other. (Amrit)

(3) [Dad, an imam] went to the mosque five times a day to lead the prayers erm and would remind me about praying and going to the mosque, but he wasn't very strict. He wasn't like, you got to get up, you haven't done this. Erm and yeah, so I think at home he was Dad, but I do understand the public-private nature of being an imam because it was erm quite public, even in our own home because most folks didn't go the see the imam erm in the mosque. Erm they erm erm would, because you remember the mosque was a house,

right it wasn't a purpose-built building, and the walls had ears, for want of a better phrase. So they would come to our house and our front room was the imam's surgery uh so they would come and talk to the imam about things. (Omar)

In talking about their childhoods, Nadia, Amrit, and Omar, all middle-aged professionals, remember places of worship being central to their experiences as children. For Nadia and Amrit, they both use 'village' to describe the community around the mosque and the gurdwara, respectively. For Nadia, the mosque serves as a place where 'everything you want' is, with care for children to seniors. In my own site visit to the mosque she attended, I was shown one of the newly constructed buildings at the site that housed the necessary equipment for preparing a dead body for burial, including a large refrigeration unit and room purpose-built for the washing of a dead body, all done by volunteers from the mosque as an act of service to their community. The mosque in this case, and in many other cases throughout the city, also includes schools where students can study both the Qur'an as well as tuition for exams. The storyline is one of complete support for those who are members of the mosque, often only paying a small fee to be a part of the community.

Amrit talks in a similar way about the gurdwara, extending the 'village' metaphor to include a 'quite rich extended family', rich here referring to the kinds of people who are a part of the community, the diversity of that group, rather than their financial status. The FAMILY metaphor becomes literal as she speaks about the community, saying that her actual family, who were also a part of that community, served as a set of role models for her and she could see the possibilities available to her through their experiences. The 'village' then comes to represent familial connections and the 'city' to represent possibility and progress, and she sees both as having had a positive influence on her.

Omar also sees a close relationship between family and religious life, in part because his father was the local imam and therefore the mosque was also their family home, and when people came to see his father, he would be there. The 'imam's surgery' is used to compare a medical GP surgery where patients access general health advice and care in the UK to spiritual care, and positions his father, the imam, in a storyline of service to the community wherein he cares for the needs of others. In his description of his living situation and his position in his family, his understanding of the connection between religious life and service, and his own personal life and space, become very closely related. The community that he is a part of is not then something that exists outside of the house, but something that he lives within, and a place into which people are regularly coming to meet with his father.

In all three of these stories about religious places of worship, the participants spoke proudly and fondly of the role of the mosque and the gurdwara at the centre of the life of the community. In several of the interviews about family histories, participants spoke of their families moving to different places within England because of the location of a place of worship where they were moving and the importance of being near particularly a mosque or gurdwara appeared central in how they represented the thinking of the generation that first came to the country, when they could make decisions about where they might live. Among the participants for whom immigration was less key to their own story, the locations of places of worship in these same ways (particularly this metaphor of a 'village') was not a common theme but not entirely absent, as Charles, an Anglo-Catholic man who was a long-time attendee of a particular church, also spoke about the importance of a church building in how he decided where to settle and worship after completing his studies.

The connection to communities extended beyond physical locations to connections based on shared values, language, or shared emotional experiences. Esther spoke about these different connections in describing a Catholic community.

(4) I think like with people who are like, who are still practising, it's, it's more like shared community. I think there's also just like the community people who were raised Catholic but don't really see themselves as Catholic anymore. And a lot of that is just like of like swapping stories, and just being like, oh yeah, you did this, yeah, we did, and just like that kind of thing. And just like, and often like it's just talking about the shared frustrations, or things like that. Erm I think it's-it's like, There is a, I remember someone saying that there is actually a thing that like, being a Catholic you can't quit. (Esther)

The connection that Esther describes is not an easily articulated relationship between a religious belief and an ongoing religious identity, but rather sees connections emerge from having grown up in the same contexts or having had similar strong emotional experiences. For Esther, these connections with her past religious identity continue to play a role in her life, as she sees connections with other former Catholics and recognises the relationships that exist between how she sees the world now and how she grew up. As she says, being Catholic is not something you could 'quit' because there is a community of people who have had similar experiences and see the world in a similar way, regardless of whether they are practising.

Throughout the interviews, people did speak about the importance of spiritual leaders within their faith communities in building and maintaining those communities, including their own parents (Omar, Michaela, Esther), gurus (Amrit, Priya), and elders (Abdul). These leaders, however, were not foregrounded in any of the stories that were told and none of the participants spoke at length about the influence of specific leaders on their own religious beliefs. Leaders could also be explicitly absent but still play important roles in how people positioned themselves when they described their experiences, as in Catherine's reflection in the previous section that she now sees her experience in the evangelical church she attended as 'manipulation', making the action a noun without identifying an actor when she describes that manipulation.

Instead, particularly in the interviews with participants who also told stories of family immigration, religious identity and belief was positioned as simply a part of who they are, and a constant in their lives. This may be an effect of the interview questions, however, which focused on participants' experiences and did not explicitly ask them to identify people who had been influential in their lives. At the same time, a focus on religious experience did not more frequently elicit stories about the influence of individuals in their lives and tended more towards memories of community. Physical, local communities of people who shared similarities beyond only religious belief and practice, time and again was the thing that participants in the study referred to in discussing their own experiences and how they came to be the person they are.

Changing Community

With all the focus on community in the lives of the participants, another consistent theme was that the communities changed over time, and that different circumstances, often outside of the control of the community and in places far away from Birmingham, could influence the day-to-day lives of individuals and the possible positions available to them and how they came to understand their own identity. The most obvious, and the one often at the forefront of negative media narratives about immigrants, is assimilation and how participants whose families had migrated to Britain in the recent past understood themselves as 'British' and felt they were accepted in this country.

(5) So, so, if I feel British and my dad. So, my daughter, um, she is now, she was first born. She's 32 years old. She's 32. So, she-she's, she feels British. She's an, I think she's a social worker. She works, but, um, yes, she feels British. She, um, does she get racism? She has now and then, but not as much as how I-I got it. So, yes. So, if I tell her, what, are you British? Well, what do I say to her? What are first? Are you British, or are you Bangladeshi? So, she says, first she's a Muslim, then she's a British, then she's a Bangladeshi. . . . With me-with me,

I am a Muslim first, then I would say I'm a Bangladeshi, then I say I'm a British. Or, with her own choice, her British comes second. (Hajrah)

(6) My kids are third-generation Bangladeshi, British-Bangladeshis. Erm their-their first language is English. My mother tongue is Bengali. So in one generation, it was the shift, you could see the change. So change is inevitable, it will happen. Erm my-my oldest, he could speak a bit of Bengali, my younger two cannot speak a single word, you know and that's in one generation. (Shabina)

(7) So in-in a way, my parents never identified themselves, as, other than ticking a box in a form, that they follow Islam or they're Muslim. They never sort of introduced themselves and-and my mother would never say, I'm a Muslim woman, she would have said, I'm a Bangladeshi woman. So that would have been her identity. I-I probably when I introduce myself, I say I'm a Brummie and I say I'm a Muslim female. My kids would probably do the same. (Shabina)

These three quotes show how religious and national identity within immigrant communities and for the children of immigrants is not necessarily straightforward, both because of their own feelings about themselves and the positions they can take within their contexts. Importantly, the discussion is not about nationality as an empirical marker of citizenship – all the participants in the study were presumably British, and none gave indications in the interviews that they did not have British citizenship. Instead, the conversations included language about 'feeling', as in extract (5) where Hajrah reports that her daughter 'feels' British and the 'feeling' of being British is contrasted with experiencing racism, positioning Britishness and one's ability to be perceived as British as being intrinsically related to one's ethnic or racial identity. Being 'Muslim' is also relevant in Hajrah's description of herself and her daughter in relation to nationality, as she positions both herself and her daughter as first Muslim and then British.

For Shabina, language plays an important role in how national identity is felt and the fact that her children speak English as a first language makes them British-Bangladeshi, something that she contrasts with her identity, where her first language is Bengali. The relationship between national identity and religious identity is also made relevant in Shabina's interview because, in addition to the discussion about national identity, like Hajrah, being Muslim is also relevant to the discussion. Comparing herself, her children, and her parents, Shabina notes that her mother would not have seen her Muslim identity as relevant in the same way that Shabina and her children do. The quote shows that generational shifts can move in different directions, and the identity of 'Muslim' is not something that her parents would have necessarily used themselves. Being immigrants to the UK, national identity could be seen as more relevant in some contexts than one's religious identity. Shabina also draws in an additional identity marker, being 'Brummie' (i.e. from Birmingham) rather than being 'British'. In this case, the local identity of Birmingham better positions Shabina in terms of her 'Britishness' because throughout the interview, Birmingham has been established as a diverse place where she grew up and feels the most connection.

Historical circumstances were also important in participant stories about their identity and how it shifted over their lives. For several of the Muslim participants, both in the interviews and in my site visits, terrorism and particularly the attack on the World Trade Center in New York City on 11 September 2001, was an important point in their lives when they came to feel they were positioned differently in British society and subsequently felt their own self-positioning change. Three examples of this follow:

(8) So that, after 9/11, your-your Muslim-hood preceded you way before you entered the room. (Omar)

(9) And I was involved in the Labour Party as well, in some aspects. And, uh, and then 9/11 took, took place, and being a Muslim student officer, being a young British Muslim, I ended up doing a lot of interviews for media. Um, Radio Four, BBC, Radio Four, various news outlets. And the world changed. The world did change, and Muslim-ness came to the forefront. Uh, whereas before it wasn't Muslim-ness, it was more about, yeah, I'm-I'm a British Indian with, sort of, a Muslim background. And we, we knew about Muslim-ness and Islamophobia, and what was happening, but-but it wasn't there at the forefront. Um, it was more, um, in the background, if you know what I mean. (Abdul)

(10) For me, my, you know, sort of when I reflect back, since 9/11, you know being a visible Muslim, you know those conversations has, I think we've, we've gone back in terms of, you know having that conversation. I'm-I'm a lot more conscious of my religion now than I was growing up, yeah you know erm and I'm a lot more aware about it. (Shabina)

In these three interviews, 9/11 was mentioned without any description of the particulars of the attacks, where they occurred, or how exactly the event itself was experienced and talked about within the community. Instead, the date becomes a metonymy for not only the events themselves, but a point where collective and individual experiences of the society changed. Omar refers to 'Muslim-hood' and

Abdul says 'Muslim-ness' to describe the part of their identity that was highlighted, encompassing a larger concept than simply a religious belief or practice. Shabina speaks more directly about being 'more conscious of her religion' in the post-9/11 world. She also refers to 'conversations', particularly as a 'visible Muslim', suggesting that she has had some specific engagement about her Muslim identity because of what she wears, and other parts of the conversation have included a discussion of the hijab and how she felt she and other women wearing the hijab have been targeted for harassment or made to feel uncomfortable in public, although in this case there doesn't appear to be a particularly negative valence when talking about these conversations.

Shabina's mention of 'having that conversation' is similar in a way to Abdul's story of being asked to be interviewed in various different places following 9/11 because he was 'a young British Muslim'. There is little detail given to what these interviews covered, but there is an implied link between the attacks and Muslim identity. Abdul goes on to describe this as bringing Muslim identity to the 'forefront', first describing himself as being a British Indian person with a Muslim background, where his national and ethnic identity was the primary way he was identified before 9/11, something that was also mentioned by Shabina, and saying that both 'Muslim-ness' and 'Islamophobia' were in the background prior to 9/11.

Although Abdul's description of both 'Muslim-ness' and 'Islamaphobia' coming to the forefront as the result of 9/11 suggests that the awareness of Islam included racism and discrimination, positive descriptions of a shift in personal and community awareness of religious identity are also present. These are not always described as the result of 9/11 – Shabina describes a generational shift in awareness of religious identity and Nadia also describes as shifting in her lifetime, highlighted in her own daughter's increased confidence in asserting her religious commitments when, in her example, asked to change how she dressed while serving in a medical context. In all of these cases, the participants described a change in the way they viewed their own religious identity in the British context and how engagement with that belief by those outside of the community had increased.

The positioning of 9/11 as a turning point and discussions of changing views of religious identity were part of a storyline wherein both Muslims and non-Muslims in the country have become more aware of Islam in British life. While the stories of participants like Hajrah and Shabina may suggest a storyline that they had been implicitly treated as non-British, this was never explicitly stated in any of the interviews. Moreover, none of the white participants positioned themselves either in terms of their ethnicity or religious beliefs, as it related to Britishness. Discussing the relationship between Christianity and British identity, Margaret, who doesn't claim any particular religious affiliation, says:

(11) For me, I don't identify Britain as being a Christian country or England as being a Christian country, that's not how I . . . how I think about us. Um, yeah. I think . . . When I think of England, I think of somewhere of diversity and of lots of different ethnicities, faith paths, traditions. Um, I-I don't identify as us being a Christian country, but I suppose that it's-it's . . . It . . . There are still elements of it that's very much woven within. (Margaret)

For Margaret, describing the United Kingdom, or 'Britain' or 'England' as a 'Christian country' is not accurate, and she positions 'England' as a 'diverse' place with 'different ethnicities, faith paths, and traditions' while still recognising that 'elements' of the Christian past are 'woven' into it. This description of Britain most explicitly reveals what is unsaid in much of the talk about Britain and British identity that emerged in the interviews: that the country is diverse and full of people of many different backgrounds, but that Christianity and Christian belief, and 'whiteness', to the extent that it is associated with that Christian belief historically, could remain part of how Britishness is understood by the population, even if people don't necessarily accept or want it to be.

Reflecting on the shift in demographics in the country and what it means to be British, Michaela talks about how the attitudes of the Black community have shifted and how new positionings have emerged since she was a child in the 1980s:

(12) We're now looking at getting along with you know Afghanis, do you get what I mean the Afghanistans [Afghanis] that are now coming in. We're getting, completely different because we're British now. Before, these children were Caribbean. These children were South Asian and they were placed in Britain amongst white working class people which made them different. Forty years later, we've got a-an entitlement to a British identity that would make me, sitting next to another Asian, a Asian girl, exactly the same age as me, do you get me, born in the same era, both went to [local school name]. We'll probably be more politically aligned now than we have ever been, and we can still be two completely different religions, but the political climate means that we've got other enemies now. We've got other ways of looking at who's an insider and who is an outsider. (Michaela)

Michaela's response shows how demographic changes over time can lead to changes in storylines about identity and how groups who previously understood the other as different have come to see each other as closely related because of their shared experiences, in this case growing up in the same neighbourhood and attending the same school. Michaela refers to this new positioning as being 'politically aligned', particularly with new immigrants arriving from Afghanistan and a realisation that 'forty years later' they have 'an entitlement to a British identity'. She also notes that part of the alignment has resulted from having 'other enemies', which she suggests comes from new ways of seeing 'who's an insider and who is an outsider'.

New immigrant communities, even those with shared beliefs, can lead to changes to how people view their own Britishness and their approach to their own religious belief. For Asian Muslim communities, the increase in Somalian Muslim immigrants could challenge how they understand Muslim identity and the importance of 'culture' in how people talk about their own religious beliefs: Shabina says:

(13) Sometimes we take those culture, people interchange between culture and religion, which for me is something so different, you know because I could be a Muslim from an Arab background, to Pakistani, to you know white, to African, you know and there's, there are five, six continents. (Shabina)

Shabina's response here shows the limitations of the understanding of 'Muslim-ness' that Abdul had noted in extract (9), because different communities come to the country with different understandings of who they are. To view 'Arab' and 'African' Muslims as essentially the same is problematic because of the cultural influence on the expression of religious identity. For the Muslim communities who have lived in Birmingham for many years, and several generations being 'Brummie', this asserts an identity that is not only British, but a particular regional British identity. As Aisha asserts by recounting the amount of time her family has spent in Birmingham, new immigrant communities, Muslim or not, come with a different set of values and understandings of what it means to be Muslim and how that identity interacts with a national identity. This contrast reinforces how families like Aisha's are a part of a British story, one that, despite the presence of Islamophobia that Abdul highlights, is and has always been present in daily life, largely accepted as British. Aisha's need to assert her identity as a Brummie, however, suggests that counter-narratives and the persistence of white supremacy in British society is still felt by those from minority religions and people of colour.

Serving Community

Despite demographic changes that suggest the United Kingdom continues to grow more secular, the participants in the Superdivercity project often made links between the work of religious organisations, both from their own communities and from other communities, and healthy civic life in the city. For the participants in the study, and particularly the links that were made through community organising, almost all of the participants told stories that in one way or another positioned their own religious communities in a storyline of serving the greater good. This included religious communities as serving those who were a part of their organisations and also members of the local community, the use of religious organisation resources and spaces to serve the community, and emerging new roles for religious organisations that had changed over time.

Throughout the project, making clear distinctions between a religious and local community proved difficult because churches, mosques, synagogues, and gurd-waras were positioned as local community institutions often before they were positioned as religious establishments. The services provided in terms of religious belief and practice were often backgrounded, and religiosity and community engagement were positioned as different things, which could be aligned, but not necessarily, as evidenced in Naomi discussing a family member's engage-ment with a religious community: 'She's more engaged with the community. Whether she's more religious ... ', leaving the rest of the sentence uncompleted. The ellipsis at the end of the statement suggests that religious commitment and community involvement were not necessarily the same thing, and with many participants community work done in and with religious organisations was not necessarily an indication of strongly held beliefs.

Instead, participants often positioned the religious organisations as deeply integrated in the work of the community, in some cases with difficulty distin-guishing between the two as in the following example.

(14) It is-is quite linked together. It's-it's-it's when you go to the mosque, you're meeting everyone, you-you know, after the prayer. And then, it's a community, it's-it's-it's a community, like, it's like a community centre, to be fair. And then, if they want to do something, you know, um, pray, we'll always have a gathering. They have, um, like, um, a tour. They will eat food. They will have a, you know, eat food. Um, that's what a gathering is, yes? And we all have, sometimes we have women's sessions. So, I, at the same time, when the, so say, if the women, men are downstairs, sometimes the women are upstairs, and we'll have a little discussion and talk about things, and have food. So, like again, like again, advice community centre. (Hajrah)

Here, Hajrah describes the role of a mosque as serving more than simply a religious purpose, and operating instead as a kind of 'community centre'. Hajrah's story includes talking about the role her father played in the commu-nity as an elder (a story that both Shabina and Omar told as well), providing support for many people in a variety of ways, and serving as an example in the local community by providing for the physical needs of recent immigrants, from immigration advice to help applying for bank accounts to renting and buying homes in the local area. This was also integrated with spiritual and ethical advice, with the elders meeting the physical and spiritual needs of the community and, at first, their homes, and later their mosques, serving as the location for those services. In their positioning, religious service and practical service were deeply integrated as a part of the immigrant experience and community leadership. Omar, as we saw in extract (3), talked about his father as an imam hosting a 'surgery'. Like Shabina and Hajrah's descriptions of their father's service, there is no distinction between the local and religious communities, and the help and support provided by imams and elders cannot be easily delineated as spiritual and practical advice.

The role of religious organisations in education and in participants' memories of growing up in religious communities was a part of many of my site visit conversations, particularly with places of worship which were connected to schools, including churches, mosques, and gurdwaras. The effect of religion in education came up in interviews about people's religious identities, but not always in straightforward ways. Three responses illustrate the different ways that religion interacted with education in talk about religious identity:

(15) I went to uh an Islamic private school, independent school, and uh
    I studied a number of subjects that you don't get to study in a kind of
    evening madrassa in a mosque because there's not much time. So in
    a madrassa in a mosque, they teach you how to erm read the Qu'ran and
    learn about your parents, but in the Islamic school, they-they covered other
    subjects, like *fiqh* [Islamic law] and Islamic history and-and other things.
    So that had a profound impact because I had people who were teaching me
    about my faith who weren't my dad. (Omar)

(16) The vicar of the, the local C of E [Church of England] church would come
    to our primary school and would come to our secondary school, and we'd
    go to church for Christmas hymn services. (Catherine)

(17) I actually went to the Catholic school, as a Muslim, which was really
    interesting because there weren't any Muslims in my Catholic school.
    (Aisha)

Omar's response shows how religious education can be a core part of upbringing and play an important role in shaping the way that a religious person might come to understand their faith, through explicit, institutional educational contexts. The other two responses, however, suggest the different ways that religion can be positioned in storylines of development of identity. Catherine recalls the presence of a vicar at school and presumably some experiences of collective worship as a child, where going to church was a part of a primary school experience in the UK, something that is not positioned as being out of the ordinary. Aisha's brief description of her experience in school, by contrast, positions her as the only Muslim in a Catholic school, something she says was 'interesting', and part of a larger positioning in her interview as being out of place as the only Muslim in a predominately white context.

Religious diversity, and how schools of religious character interact with people of different faiths, often through the discussion of shared values, has been a theme in previous research I've done with colleagues on Church of England schools which serve predominately Muslim communities (Pihlaja et al., 2022). Stories about regular, positive engagement with people of other faiths also can develop into storylines of shared values and mutual understanding. These interactions can be positioned as helping one understand one's own faith. Allen, for example, a Quaker, recounted how a Muslim classmate was inspired to engage with his own faith through the practice of silence in a Quaker school. Examples like these show how interactions with people of different faiths can be understood to motivate self-understanding.

Other examples of community involvement included more implicit interactions between religious organisations and their local communities. Shabina, as an organiser working with women, predominantly with a Muslim user population, positioned the work of the organisation as teaching skills that don't necessarily explicitly engage with religious belief. Shabina says:

(18) Erm so you know on a Monday, we do sewing, the ladies come and they sew. But that's just a way of getting them together. On the Tuesday is traditionally what we call a coffee morning. Erm, you know, so you, the ladies will come. And more or less last week knew this talk [occurring at the centre that day] was happening. Next week, there's a winter project where we'll talk about Covid and a bit about you know preparing for winter. . . . So our engagement, some of the activities we do are almost erm is secondary. It's just a tool of getting them together. Erm it's those conversations we have, the unpacking, erm providing I think that safe space, is almost the most important part for us as a, as an organisation and how do we actually you know enable them to erm reach their f-full potential as an individual. (Shabina)

In Shabina's description, the focus is on building community, with the practical skills that are developed being 'almost . . . secondary'. Here, religious identity is backgrounded in a storyline of helping people 'reach their full potential as an individual'. Religious organisations also offer material support in terms of housing community organisations, as Margaret, a community organiser with no religious affiliation, works for the Methodist Church in a building owned and operated by a non-denominational international church. In both of these contexts, the presence of support from religious individuals and organisations, even in serving people of the same religious belief, does not position religious belief and practice as the focus of the work but rather foregrounds community and personal development.

These storylines of service and the positioning of the mosques, churches, and gurdwaras as central locations presented an understanding of religious and community life as deeply integrated, with little separation between the spiritual and physical needs of those in the community. Instead, the communities and the religious institutions within them were a part of a single understanding of life in the city. Speaking about belief and religious practices was not separate from the life of the community, and even in talk about separation from religious belief, as in Esther's talk about her Catholic upbringing and her own adult identity apart from that upbringing, the church and Catholic community still remained a part of her life that she recognised.

The positioning of participants in a close relationship between religious and community life was in many ways the result of the participants who were interviewed. They were often civically engaged and religious, with a clear interest in their religious communities being seen as actively committed to making the local community a better place. How this positioning represents all or most or a majority of any individual community might be difficult to discern, but it plays a crucial role in how communities understand themselves and how they are positioned by those around them, particularly in contexts where discrimination continues to persist. This positioning, as a public representation of what is important to them, leads to real relationships between people of different faiths and organisations. They create storylines of engagement in civic life that benefit those religious communities in perpetuating a perception of religious believers as tolerant and willing to work with others.

Conclusion

Community was at the heart of participants' positioning and storylines about religious identity. As people positioned themselves in relation to religious belief and practice, the life of the community in which they were often also raised, with long histories of involvement in religious organisations that were central to local life, was important in talking about what their religious identity meant to them. Stories about the religious communities and their own involvement in those communities were used to explain what it meant to be a member of a religious faith. The histories of those communities, particularly in the case of immigrants, was important in shaping how they saw themselves, but participants also recognised the importance of changing social dynamics and history, whether it be in global events like the terrorist attacks on 9/11 or shifting demographics in a particular area, on how they were able to position themselves, often seeing those shifts in complicated ways. Religious identity and community life were deeply integrated elements in individual storytelling and because of the close relationships among people of different faiths in the community, the two positionings as a Brummie and a religious person were often closely related.

Living Superdiversity

This Element began by noting that unease about changing demographics in places like Birmingham has been an ongoing part of media narratives in the UK. At the same time, research into linguistic superdiversity has shown that the media narratives of segregated communities living in an isolated way are erroneous (see, for example, previous work on linguistic diversity in Birmingham: Blackledge & Creese, 2020; Creese & Blackledge, 2019) and, indeed, the analysis so far has shown how people of all different religious backgrounds view themselves as members of an integrated society. This final analysis section will look at storylines of diversity that emerged in talk about the city and how it is experienced: how participants see diversity in their day-to-day experiences, how racism and prejudice occur, and how they interact with people from other faiths in civic life. Please note that some of the quotes in this section include racial slurs that are reproduced as the participants used them in describing the racism that members of their community have experienced.

The Superdiverse City

Throughout the interviews and site visits, diversity in Birmingham was almost always presented in a positive light and one of the main strengths of the city. The storylines around diversity, particularly when participants talked about their engagement with people of different faiths, were positive. When there was discussion of tensions or racism, participants told stories wherein negative experiences were the exception, and even these stories were often parts of larger storylines of acceptance and peace. For example, in a site visit to a Shi'a mosque, I was told about an incident of sectarian vandalism and graffiti in the prayer hall. However, this incident was positioned as leading to increased cooperation between the mosque and other Sunni mosques in the area, condemning sectarian violence, and followed up quickly with a story of different mosques supporting one another to open Covid-19 vaccination centres. In all of these stories, a storyline of faith leaders working together to tackle different obstacles emerged: there could be difficulties, but they were often overcome.

Rather than interfaith dialogue about theological issues, participants in this project often talked about examples of taking part in religious ceremonies and events hosted by people of other faiths. Christian participants reported taking part in Ramadan celebrations, and during the project local universities hosted different community iftars for people of all faiths, including the progressive synagogue in Birmingham hosting a multi-faith Iftar and inviting Muslim participants to use their sanctuary for prayers before breaking their fast. At these events, people of different faiths, ethnicities, ages, genders, sexual orientations, citizenship statuses, and other markers of diversity spoke in positive ways about the benefits of the diversity and acceptance on them as individuals and their communities more generally.

These were practical examples of how stories of acceptance and the benefits of diversity could be paired with events that then would bring together communities in a spirit of peace and shared values. The same examples of positive positioning of communities in diverse areas and their positive effect on people of faith could also be seen in the interviews, for example, where Alexandra spoke of moving to Birmingham:

(1) I love Birmingham, the [unclear], the multiculturalism and the yeah, it is just fantastic, I think, and Cumbria was so different. West Yorkshire, where I was before, was different as well because it was, well it was diverse, but it wasn't mixed very much. You could see this is a white area and this is an Asian area. Yes, you can see this here as well, but the mixture is so much better and diversity is better and wider, it's not just Asian or just Black, it's everybody. Um, so yeah, that rubs off on the churches. They can't survive, they can't, we have small, white-only churches in an Asian area because they've been there for 200 years and the Asians have been there for, I don't know, fifty years or so, so yeah, they are still there and they don't mix, because they're surrounded by Muslims. I find it, yeah, I don't know whether to laugh or to cry, but I think why don't you mix, you know? (Alexandra)

Alexandra makes the distinction between diversity in which people live in segregated spaces and Birmingham where she sees people more 'mixed', although she does note that some segregation still occurs. Importantly, she notes that this 'rubs off on the churches', without making explicit what this influence specifically entails. She then goes on to recount how the changes in demographics and specifically the increase in immigrant populations from Muslim and 'Asian' backgrounds have led to situations where some churches have adapted and engaged, and others have not. She describes her response as being unsure whether 'to laugh or cry', to find their lack of engagement with their communities so absurd that it's comical or to despair at their lack of willingness to work with those around them.

Like Alexandra noted in describing how shifts in demographics led to 'white' churches in predominately 'Asian' communities, in several site visits and interviews I spoke with religious community members who had seen a significant drop off in engagement with their local community and for whom the role of the religious had shifted over time and necessitated a shift in thinking about the purpose of religious organisations. For example, one Anglo-Catholic participant who served in a leadership position in his church describes witnessing great demographic change: 'The most recent census says that over 70 per cent of the population in the parish boundaries are . . . identify as either Muslim or other world faiths other than Christianity.' This shift has led to only one parishioner who lives in the parish boundaries, and reflecting on the size of their community over the years, he says:

(2) And um, we [the executive team] occasionally among ourselves talk about, about the future and we're all realistic and we say, well, we have absolutely no idea what this church will be doing in twenty-five or thirty or fifty years' time. But our job is to keep it going for the moment. (Charles)

The discussion of the church's position in this case relates to both the demographic changes in the area and the specific position of Anglo-Catholicism in modern Britain and ongoing disagreements about the role of women in the church. The church's physical and theological position led to a situation wherein the numbers of parishioners have waned, in part because of fewer people in the local community, but also in part because new immigrant communities have not replaced the white congregation as immigrants have in other contexts in the city, including in Evangelical Christian and Catholic communities. Charles notes that demographic change can 'go both ways' and although they have seen a decline in participation in recent years, this does not necessarily mean it will continue and, as he notes, the team's job is to 'keep it going for the moment'.

In light of these reflections, Charles goes on to discuss the role of the church and its position as serving those in the parish, and he gives two examples. The first is telling the story of the church's clock tower:

(3) But there was a period of about a year when the clock was not going and Muslim, um, members of the public who live locally told us that it was an inconvenience for them that the clock was not working because they relied upon the clock to remind them of the [unclear] prayer. (Charles)

The second example is the use of the church's hall by people of all different faiths for various events, including for a boxing club and which, Charles notes, provides the opportunity for young women, including young Muslim women, to develop self-discipline and train together with young men. The positioning of the church in this role, offering training and unique experiences for young women, fits into a storyline of the church offering opportunity and transformation to the community, but not in an explicitly religious way.

Charles' stories about the church's interaction with Muslims, and these two examples, underscore how changes in demographics lead to new positions for religious communities, and how seemingly small interactions between people of different faiths can emerge as meaningful in storylines about living together and cooperating. Although both examples represent seemingly small series of interactions, their importance in the church community's understanding of themselves and their value suggests that changes in demographics and religious attendance are also opportunities for organisations to see new roles for themselves and rethink how resources are allocated to serve those around them.

Charles' discussion of the experience of their church shows how community understandings of one another are not necessarily straightforwardly positive, and can involve two communities living in the same space without necessarily engaging with one another. How Charles sees the value of the church is then informed by his own understanding of the culture of those living in the parish. At the same time, with the exception of the use of the church hall, Charles did not have any stories of people from the Muslim community coming and seeking to build a relationship with the church. Charles, then, understands how the church is viewed by others not through interaction with local Muslims, but through imagining the perspective of those Muslims.

Like Charles, many of the participants in the project were members of minority religious groups, or minorities within larger groups such as Shi'a Muslims in a predominately Sunni Muslim population, or Quakers or Catholics in a context where the Church of England is still the dominant Christian denomination. For Christians like David, who attends a Congregationalist church and is a physicist, living with people of different beliefs involves accepting that there are complexities to what individuals believe and, as discussed in the section on self-identity, 'staying quiet' when disagreeing about specific parts of the creed. A similar statement about how interreligious relationships can be managed with care taken to what one says and when it is said comes from Priya, a Sikh woman of Indian descent. She speaks about her relationship with her white British husband and how she deals with the complications of having different faiths and how to raise the children in light of their differences:

(4) To some extent I suppose, which I deliberately tried to keep it, you know, general, most of the time … In order to, um, not, um, uh … What's the word? Uh, um, not alienate my husband. (Priya)

Then speaking of her children she says:

(5) So, so they've grown up with what I've told them. You know, I read the bible, we read the bible together, you know … and are happy to encompass it all. Um, but what you can't get away from is that, you know, ultimately we believe in a master who is the son of god, and which, you know, for somebody who doesn't believe, that's very difficult. Um, so, so again I tend not to focus on that massively. (Priya)

In this portion of the interview, there is an increase in hedging and a carefully worded discussion of the relationship with her husband and, in particular, how to deal with differences in religious belief between the two. She describes her own belief but also the need to not 'alienate' her husband. She describes her efforts to relate to Christian faith through reading the bible, but notes the limits of that engagement when it comes to the core difference in the faiths: 'we believe in a master who is the son of God' and notes that this is 'difficult' for people who don't believe. The 'we' in the sentence is ambiguous, but seems to imply that she and her children hold the same belief, whereas her husband does not, and her response to this difference is 'not to focus on that'.

Priya's discussion of her interreligious relationship highlights a kind of difficult topic of conversation that may have been absent from the data in part because of the positive focus of the research and the public positioning of interfaith relationships in positive storylines of peace and acceptance. However, these stories of living and working together, and testimonies about acceptance at interfaith events, are told in balance with negative story-lines that are prominent not only in media but also in the communities themselves. While leaders, and many of the participants were in leadership positions in various civic and religious organisations, are regularly telling stories of acceptance and shared values, these storylines implicitly oppose dominant negative storylines of interaction between different faiths which have long histories of violence, prejudice, and hate. They are also subject to storylines about the secularisation of British society and the waning influence of religion in the public square. The public positioning of different people of faith living together in peace is situated in this context, where changes in how religion more generally is positioned in society may necessitate a rethinking of how religious believers understand themselves no longer only as members of individual faiths but people of faith more generally, for whom there is more in common in having a shared religious belief compared to a growing population for whom religious belief is no longer important.

Racism and Tension

In the previous section, I touched on the discussion of changes to how Muslim communities were perceived following 9/11, leading to a growing awareness of Islam in British society. The effects of terrorism included both a spike in explicit Islamophobia but also an increased awareness among Muslims about their religious identity. The link between religious and national or ethnic identity did come up in other places in the interviews when, for example, Jonathan spoke of his Irish parents and the treatment of Catholics when he was a boy in the 1960s. The same suspicion of Irish immigrants was echoed in a site visit and discussion with a Catholic priest recounting the history of discrimination, and how perceptions of Irish immigrant communities shifted over the last 100 years, with the assimilation of Irish people in Birmingham.

For many participants, experiences of racism, both explicit and implicit, were reported regularly in the interviews. The following extracts come from interviews with an Asian woman and a Black woman, both telling stories related to racist behaviour they either experienced themselves or which they observed or were subsequently told about.

(6) You know, being called all sorts of names. I've been called, um, you know, usual, I won't say it now, but the usual Pakis. They use like this. You go back to your own country. Blah, blah, blah. And, you know, you just think, oh God, you know. But then that didn't strike you as racist because you think that's normal. Because they say that anyway. So, you, you just-you just-you just take it on your chin and just think, yes, you know, you-you-you thought that was normal. Forward, fifty years on, forward, forward to now, and when they say that to you now, then you just think, what has changed? (Hajrah)

(7) So, what you'll find is that that level of resistance to racism in the- in the late sixties, early seventies you know what I mean, these boys, these men have grown up- these children have grown up in, in probably one of the worst sociological times that you could actually be alive on planet earth for. An eleven-year-old to have to dodge stones and be called a nigger at the age of eleven. These are the things that they were going through, so, you know, they were heavily politicised. (Michaela)

A historical understanding of racism and its effect on the community is clear in both Hajrah and Michaela's comments here. Hajrah reports experiences of racist language which have been ongoing for her whole life, and in a storyline about the regular use of slurs she discusses how the use of racist slurs became so normalised that it was viewed as something to be simply endured, 'to take it on your chin'. At the same time, she notes that little has changed in racist behaviour over her lifetime. Michaela's description of racism and its effects on a particular generation is punctuated by the use of a racial slur and descriptions of violence to explain the conditions experienced by her parents' generation. The racist violence they experienced, Michaela then suggests, explains how a group of men came to understand themselves and their position in society, saying they became 'heavily politicised'. Michaela goes on to talk about how her upbringing in a Rastafarian household was heavily influenced by Black consciousness thinking and the need to be politically and socially aware. For her, the experience of racism is not something to endure but motivates political action to oppose larger systems of oppression.

When experiencing racism, the participants also reported their own attempts to understand the mindset of those who were acting in racist ways, often reasoning on their behalf about their actions. Two extracts here from Muslim women reflect this reasoning, with Shabina first reflecting on the importance of talking about the Superdivercity project.

(8) It's quite timely, isn't it, last you know the Yorkshire Cricket Club you know branding every-anybody that looks brown Paki. S-Sorry to use that, but I'm just using that as a you know A lot of my (laughs) non-Muslim Indian friends have been called Paki. You know so you know A racist person would never sort of differentiate whether you're Muslim, Hindu, Sikh. For them, a brown person is . a Paki or a brown person . is a brown person. So you know those differences, you know an outsider, are not able to you know differentiate between that. (Shabina)

(9) But for perception of other people, have things changed for me? I would say, no, because they don't see you as, you know, when you say you're Muslim, they'll just, some- I'm not saying everyone. But they'll just look at you thinking, oh, you know, they think, yes, they think, they probably think terrorist, or I don't know what they think. But they're probably thinking terrorist. They're probably thinking I'm ISIS. They're probably. But they don't know me, so they can't assume what I am. You know, judge me. (Hajrah)

The reasoning behind racist behaviour is disregarded in both of these extracts with characterisations of individuals who have acted in racist ways or said racist things. In the first quote, Shabina mentions the 'Yorkshire Cricket Club', referring to a news report about racist bullying and using the place as a metonymy for racist words and actions, and then relates this example to another recurring story of her friends being referred to with a racist slur. Shabina concludes this positioning of people who use racist language by saying racists 'are not able to ... differentiate' between Black and brown people of different religious backgrounds and ethnicities, saying that 'outsiders' don't differentiate between different religions of 'brown people'. Hajrah, reflecting on how things have changed over time, similarly positions 'them', the people who have treated Muslims in a negative way over the years and used racist slurs, as 'probably' understanding all Muslims as 'terrorists' or 'ISIS'. She concludes that these people 'judge me', even though they 'don't know me, so they can't assume what I am'.

The extracts so far have included instances of historical violence and prejudice leading to verbal abuse, but imminent physical violence was also a concern for some. For Naomi, a Jewish participant, threats of violence were a very real part of her experience:

(10) I think, there are those that see [synagogue] as a well-established, thriving part of a community. You know, we're very much ... You know, it is engaged in the interfaith worlds. Um, you know ... Sorry, there's something ... It's about, you know, engaging the interfaith worlds and so on. But in a ... Deep within me, the community as a whole doesn't, doesn't escape the whole antisemitism debate that's going on. The whole, Jews run the world, you know, all those tropes about power. Um, I don't know if you know that we have security outside all our synagogues ... (Naomi)

Naomi here is talking about the place of the synagogue and positions the Jewish community in Birmingham as 'a well-established, thriving part of a community'. At the same time, she mentions 'the whole antisemitism debate that's going on' and 'the whole, Jews run the world', presumably referring to how antisemitism remained in the news in a variety of different ways, including in the UK Labour Party (Staples-Butler, 2020) and the resurgence of antisemitic conspiracy theories (Allington & Joshi, 2020). She describes the feeling as something 'deep within' her that the Jewish community remains under threats of violence, linked in her story of her family and others in the synagogue of fleeing the Holocaust and coming to the UK. She then notes that the synagogue requires security, something that I experienced when attending the synagogue's multifaith iftar and notably the only time I attended an event in Birmingham where this was the case. Naomi's positioning of herself and the community as the potential object of a threat, with the historical storylines of violence against

Jewish people, shows how storylines can become embedded in understandings of religious groups, and how those storylines affect the communities themselves. The practical consequences of these storylines can be real acts of violence.

In discussions of racism in communities, how leaders and religious practitioners can address racism in religious contexts appears to also be a difficult topic to handle. Here, a church leader and a community leader both reflect on how racism can be confronted.

(11) I don't think that they're a big racist congregation. But I think they're probably not aware of their own bias. . . . I've noticed that we have always asked these people to read, maybe we should ask other people to read. You know, have you met this family, they've been coming here for a really long time, and I've never seen you talk to them. Um, I suppose just encouragement on how people reflect. But it's really tricky because, because if you say to people, you know, you haven't done this, they go, oh, you're saying I'm a racist, you know. Um, people are very fragile, and helping people think that through . . . And you don't want to take it so slowly that you actually are rejecting the people you're trying to include. (Sophie)

(12) And, this was, hang on, before the, just before the pandemic, or during, or it wasn't [unclear]. It was before the pandemic. You know, slurs, that, that's a normal thing, you know. Um, you know, Pakis go back to your home country. Go back. You know. What you, what are you doing here? And I say, look, hang on. Slow down. Calm down. I've-I've-I've a right to be here. I'm probably more British than you. I was born here. My grandchildren, my daughters. You know. I have three generations here, because I'm a grandmother. I'm a grandmother. My daughter was born here. I have grandchildren that were born here. So, you know, don't tell me, you know, to do that, you know, go back home and etc. I've heard that so many times. (Hajrah)

In discussing how institutional and implicit racism affects her church, Sophie begins by positioning her congregation as not being racist, but suggests instead that racism can appear in implicit ways, for instance in who could be chosen to speak or read in front of the congregation. She positions people as 'fragile' when it comes to these discussions, particularly when they may feel they are being positioned as a racist. Hajrah, in a different vein, also describes confronting racist behaviour by speaking directly to a person saying 'go back home' and asserting her right to be in the UK, even saying 'I'm probably more British than you'. It's not clear from her description of this sort of exchange if it has actually transpired, particularly with her use of the simple present tense 'say' and her ending the description of this encounter with 'I've heard that so many times'. The rejoinder instead suggests that the basis for the racist attack is without merit and Hajrah's response is to reassert her own identity.

In Hajrah's descriptions of 'racists' in extract (9) and in this extract, 'racists' are positioned as ignorant and lacking basic understandings about the people they are treating negatively. Hajrah's statement that they 'don't know me' suggests that the lack of understanding comes from a lack of connection with the communities that they are treating badly. Michaela, on the other hand, suggests that racism is part of a larger political project of oppression. These extracts and the larger conversation about the need for mutual understanding suggest that racism can be overcome with education and through interaction among people of different faiths; that dialogue and experiences with others can be used to combat racism because being with people you may otherwise be prejudiced against allows you to better understand who they are and why they do what they do. Presumably, then, in this understanding of interaction with diverse groups of people, seeing someone as a 'terrorist' would be much more difficult.

The discussions of racism, both considering the historical contexts and individual experiences, show how abuse and prejudice can challenge storylines of progress in relationships between groups. Although superdiversity was generally positioned as a positive thing, the challenge of racism remained a substantial concern. The examples of addressing racism by either ignoring or enduring it, challenging it on a personal level, or working to effect institutional change, all positioned racists as acting ignorantly, either because they didn't understand the culture of the people they attacked or because they were a part of a system which was inherently racist. In these storylines, racists could be stopped when people challenged them and worked to make minority communities better understood.

A Positive Presence

Throughout this Element, the positive influence of religious belief and the shared values of different faiths has been positioned as a positive force in storylines of cooperation and peace. The specifics of different beliefs and where disagreements emerged were largely absent from the talk and participants focused instead on finding the shared position that religious believers had in the city. This seemed to be, in part, due to an ability among participants to talk about their own faith in comparison to others in a way that focused on shared values rather than shared beliefs, something which my previous research with colleagues looking at Church of England primary education had found (Whisker et al., 2020). Amrit, for example, spoke about the importance of the turban in Sikh religion because it represents values that 'connect us as human beings', and is therefore something more than 'to preserve heritage'.

Shared religious belief and ethnicity could also be positioned in different ways in talk about interaction with people who might share one characteristic with you but not another, potentially leading to both connections and conflict, depending on how those differences or similarities came up in the interaction.

(13) Um, and it interestingly, I think, um, amongst East African, um, Asians, you know, uh, being neighbours with, you know, Hindus, Muslims . . . Switching between Guajarati Hindi or, to Swahili Punjabi, there was always this easy, between, uh, languages, religions, um, in that sense. (Amrit)

(14) But, but there's a lot of other challenges that come in, and I think a lot of people don't understand the challenge of immigration, the challenge of being accepted, the challenge of, um, the notion of what is home. And these kind of things can stifle communities and families as well. And it's easy to kind of say, oh, oh, the Muslims aren't, kind of, doing this, or the Muslims aren't, kind of, doing that. But, but there's, there's a lot of, there's not one single Muslim community. There's different voices. (Abdul)

In the first extract, Amrit discusses interactions among Asians who have come to the UK via East Africa and talks about how switching between languages was common among people from that area and the relationship of shared languages made interaction among the people of different faiths 'easy' in a way. By contrast, Abdul talks about how religion can be seen as a useful lens for looking at the 'Muslim community' and how Muslims should be viewed in the UK. Abdul suggests the need to think about the positioning of immigrants and how they come to understand themselves in the UK, rather than thinking that Muslims act in one way or another, with a need to recognise the 'different voices' that are a part of the community.

Both of these comments show how communities can be envisioned in different ways, and how commonalities can emerge across different groups who, for example, share the same language, while at the same time not overgeneralising about how groups see and understand themselves from an outsider's perspective. Abdul warns against the 'stifling' effect of overgeneralising about a group, Muslims in his example, and having expectations about how they are. The challenge of diversity is navigated in part by the ability to position oneself and others in different storylines at different times, thinking about oneself in terms of religious identity at some points and thinking about oneself in terms of ethnic, national, or another identity at other points. Taking on different positions in different storylines, and the ability to position others in different storylines, allows for a dynamic understanding of how people think and act in the way they do, seeing others as individuals with a variety of different identities and interests.

Storylines of coming together were not limited to shared features of identity, and shared concerns about the future and the necessity of working together to address structural issues was also a theme when it came to talking about how people of different faiths could work together because of a shared future in a world where diversity is now the norm:

(15) There's [a] faith, faith-based climate action group that's called [name of organisation], um, that Quakers are very involved in. And that, um, a lot of that is around, um, providing activities for young people. Um, so there is, so it's, I guess, the-the, um, the interactions with other faiths, ah, tend to be on, um, areas of, um, where-where there's, kind of, shared action like on, like on climate, in relation to the climate crisis and climate justice. Um, rather than being about let's have a, let's have, a-a, an interaction where we seek to understand each other's faiths. (Allen)

Allen in this extract talks about the relationship between Quakers and people of other faiths. Prompted initially for any examples of 'interreligious dialogue', he gives an example of people speaking and working together on the issues of the climate crisis and climate justice. He refers to this as a 'shared action' and contrasts that with having 'an interaction where we seek to understand each other's faiths', although the group doesn't explicitly focus on issues of faith but instead sees faith as motivating action. This story positions the two faith groups as working together on common goals rather than trying to understand one another's theological positions. Working together for climate action is, therefore, a way to 'understand each other's faiths'.

Although there were few examples of people bringing up explicit interfaith discussions about theology and belief in the interviews, my site visits and conversations with leaders did highlight some initiatives, particularly one called 'The Feast' wherein interreligious dialogue is facilitated among young people while sharing meals together and differences in faiths are explicitly addressed in discussions. For the community and religious leaders that were interviewed in the project, however, examples of interreligious engagement were more often like the one Allen describes here, where people of different faiths work together on a common goal like opening Covid-19 vaccination centres, addressing poverty, or working together on the climate crisis.

These shared interests in the wellbeing of the community and the need to make positive change can be linked together in charity work and working together for the greater good of the community, particularly through care that is motivated from the values of different religious backgrounds. Two examples of this work and the shared values that underpin them can be seen in these extracts.

(16) But I think faith erm publicly isn't, wants to be, wants to show it's there for people and help and support them. Erm, so I was, I just, before this meeting, I was with erm uh-uh Sikh leaders at the [local gurdwara]. And you know powerful what he said is that before we can start getting people to think about worship or anything or even community empowerment, you need to think about, erm I forgot the, uh-uh three words he used, erm, roti, that means food, kapda means clothes, and then, I forgot the third word, it meant shelter. (Omar)

(17) I think it's really important to understand the constraints for people working at a community level. You know it's often capacity, erm capability. And also, a power thing as well it could. Erm so that's why it's-it's important to have those larger anchor organisations, the likes of Citizens UK. Not necessarily the agency doesn't need to necessarily be local authority, it needs to be erm civil society organisations, the health providers actually providing those opportunities for these community people to come together. (Shabina)

Omar, as a Muslim, recounts something he heard from a talk at a local gurdwara and how faith should be shown in public spaces. In thinking about worship and community empowerment, the leader had said that actions must be oriented towards the core needs of a person as roti (food), kapda (clothes), and makaan (shelter), linking acts of faith and worship with care for the individual. Shabina, in discussing the role of religious and other community organisations in helping support the community, talks about community organising charities, like Citizens UK, having an important role in supporting civil society apart from the local city authority. The implication in both comments is that faith and religious belief and practice have an important role to play in how society works and that religious people in the community can and should be involved in the care and support of those around them.

Seeing the relationship between civil society organisations and individuals (both religious and non-religious), the power of the superdiverse city is the ability for people to draw on any number of different positions and storylines to better understand others, themselves, and their religious beliefs and values in relation to others. Shabina reflects on this, saying:

(18) I think as we . . . move, as we progress, I think the narrative will change.
Erm and I think in particular in a city like Birmingham, we're a super
diverse city, there's no majority, minority, you know so I think that's the
beauty of this city, such, so multicultural, you know, you could-you could
you know the world lives here. So when I think-I think it's-it's-it's you
know it's places like this, place-based you know work, you know
intervention that will actually erm allow the next generations to embrace
who they are, their identity. You know we don't necessarily need to be one
or the other, we could be several, or many, we could have many identities,
and I think that's really important. (Shabina)

The benefit of the superdiverse context is that individuals are not limited by one
way of doing things or seeing the world. Superdiversity creates a space where
different ways of being can be understood as legitimate, and no one needs to be
limited by a narrow understanding of themselves or their culture. Shabina takes
the position that multiculturalism is not only about understanding and appreci-
ating the cultures of others but seeing in others your own potential to be
different. She positions the 'next generations' in particular as benefitting from
the proximity of people living close together. The possibility is not only tolerance and peace between people with different identities but personal transformation and development.

Conclusion

Religious diversity in Birmingham and the demographic changes that the city
has experienced have become an important part of the identity of people from
the city. To be *Brummie*, as the participants said from different perspectives, is
about embracing the differences among people and seeing the community
around you as a part of your own identity. Certainly, racism, discrimination,
and violence are a part of life in the city, and negative experiences, particularly
for communities that have been historically marginalised, were a core part of the
stories that people told. The storylines about the city, however, and about the
experiences of living with people who are different from you, were largely
positive, and people positioned themselves in storylines of working with others
to bring about positive change. Moreover, the interactions with others, particularly with people who were perceived as not sharing the same beliefs as them,
could be told in storylines of learning, empathy, and personal growth, not
simply tolerance. The lives and experiences of others were resources that
anyone could benefit from to better understand themselves and to grow as
people, with new possibilities for new stories and identities to emerge in and
around them.

Conclusion: Stories and Understanding

Narrative and Religion in the Superdiverse City began with the goal of understanding the relationship between how people talked about their lives and their religious identities, with a focus on how stories and storytelling were important parts of how people positioned themselves in relation to their communities. The main findings from this Element are:

- Stories are essential for understanding who people are, both regarding their religious identity and how they see their place in civil society. People spent less time talking about beliefs when they were asked about their religious identity, and more time talking about what their community and faith tradition valued and what their experiences taught them about how they should view the world.
- Racism and discrimination are still serious problems and people from minority religious and ethnic communities, even in superdiverse contexts, are subject to stigmatisation, based largely on how they look. How the media portrays minority religious communities is still felt to be largely negative and people from minority ethnic and religious communities know that there are places they are not welcome or safe.
- Many people love diverse spaces and see everyone around them as part of their community. Even when people do not share the same religious faith, they quite often have similar values, and many organisations throughout the city are eager to work together to promote a common good and understanding. People do not want to 'keep to themselves' but to share life together.

In research into language and religious identity, this Element has shown similar themes to work by Lytra, Gregory, Souza, and colleagues (Gregory et al., 2013; Lytra et al., 2016; Souza, 2016) highlighting the close relationship between religious and cultural and ethnic identity, and the importance of language use in maintaining those identities. The way participants spoke about their religious beliefs and practices and their cultural and ethnic identities were often tied to one another, and differentiating between these identities is impossible. Different narratives may be observed in data from converts to religious beliefs, but for many people for whom religion is an important part of their identity, a relationship to their family and their own cultural and ethnic identities is key.

Throughout the project, the participants consistently focused on positive interaction in the city and the normality of interacting with people from different backgrounds. Gilroy (2004) has described the 'conviviality' of life in multicultural contexts, that is, the 'everyday practices of multi-ethnic interaction' that Valluvan notes have become 'unremarkable' (2016, p. 218). The persistence of racism in the experience of many in the dataset, however, highlights Noronha's (2022) warning that 'racist cultures and practices which structure the cities and societies being studied' (p. 160) need to be properly theorised to work with notions of conviviality. This same sentiment can be found in a comment made by the participant Michaela that people who previously might have seen themselves as different might have more in common with one another because of where they've grown up and because 'we've got other enemies now'. The practices of living in multicultural and subsequently multireligious places is not, even in superdiverse contexts, free from pernicious and persistent structural and individual racist ideologies and actions.

This Element has shown the centrality of narrative in religious identity and in how people understand themselves and interact with others. That narrative construction of identity is a process that follows the trajectory of the interaction. Though there is no evidence in this dataset that people represent themselves in contradictory ways, the data showed that whether and how one presents a religious identity depends on the discourse context. This is not to downplay or ignore the importance of belief in the religious identities of the participants and indeed research like Bhatt (2023), Rumsby and Eggert (2023), and Butt (2023) show how co-religionist and autoethnographic research can perhaps better capture the internal experiences of religious belief as they relate to identity. Still, the public presentation of belief, faith, and religious identity revealed in this Element has consequences for how religious identity is then approached in contexts of religious diversity, in that context is consequential to how people talk about their experience and religious identity. If care can be taken to the context and trajectory of conversation, very different outcomes might emerge in contexts that might otherwise be confrontational.

Thinking about these findings and considering how they could be used to help people better talk about their faith and the faiths of others, I developed a five-step resource to guide people in starting to talk about their faith, presented as an infographic to be distributed in the different organisations (see Figure 1). The model is built on a core tool of community organising, the one-to-one, where organisers set up intentional conversations to better understand the self-interests of people in their communities. The goal of this resource was to help educators, teachers, and religious leaders encourage talk about faith in different contexts. The model is:

1. **Relax.** Everyone has different ideas and beliefs about the world. Celebrate who you are and don't worry about what others will think.
2. **Tell your story.** What you think and believe is a part of your unique experience. Don't be afraid to tell people about what you've experienced.

Figure 1 How should we talk about our beliefs?

3. **Be curious.** Just like you, everyone else has their own story. Listen to what they have to say and ask questions.
4. **Find common ground.** Even though we're different, we often have a lot in common. Look for the similarities in others.
5. **Change your mind.** It's okay to change what you think. Let new experiences affect how you see the world.

For practitioners in civil society organisations, the model creates an agenda for discussion about faith and invites people to talk about their own life experiences with one another instead of focusing on articles of faith or esoteric issues. It encourages people to think about others' experiences and ask and answer questions to better understand the other person while looking for things that they have in common. The model doesn't include any trick to helping people talk about faith, and indeed can be used to talk with anyone – its use is not limited to people with religious differences, or even any differences. The goal is simply to facilitate conversations that encourage people to think about how another person's perspective is motivated by their lived experience.

Religious diversity offers people the opportunity to better understand themselves and others, but these benefits can only be felt when people start to talk openly and frequently about what they value and how values are shared in a community. In the dataset explored in this Element, the experience of life with people who shared different beliefs, cultures, and experiences was almost always talked about with a sense of joy, excitement, and energy, something that permeates the culture of the city. When talking about negative experiences, and in particular when talking about racism, the participants stressed the lack of understanding they sensed from people that attacked them. Shabiba's comment that racists can't tell the difference between people of different ethnicities and faith, and Hajrah's exasperation with people misunderstanding citizenship and her own family's long history in the city, suggests that conflict emerges first from a lack of understanding of others' lived experiences. Simply understanding others will not solve racism, but it is a necessary starting point. They must be understood in systems of oppression which result in structural disadvantages (Gholami, 2021).

The 'Language and Religion in the Superdiverse City' project showed the transformative potential of coming to understand yourself in a diverse space and seeing the differences around you not as a threat to your own autonomy but a way to better understand your own values. The stories that we tell, and the storylines that emerge out of the diversity of voices, create the world that we live in, and as David Graeber writes, 'The ultimate, hidden truth of the world is that it is something that we make, and could just as easily make differently.' The challenge to move past racism and injustice and discrimination, when met and overcome, leads to individuals and communities who see in others, in people who don't necessarily look or act or believe as they do, the potential for a shared future where difference is celebrated and transforms the world around them.

References

Abrams, D., & Hogg, M. (2010). Social identity and self-categorization. In J. Dovidio, M. Hewstone, P. Glick, & V. Esses (Eds.), *The Sage handbook of prejudice, stereotyping and discrimination* (pp. 179–193). Sage.

Al-Hejin, B. (2015). Covering Muslim women: Semantic macrostructures in BBC News. *Discourse & Communication*, *9*(1), 19–46. https://doi.org/10.1177/ 1750481314555262.

Allington, D., & Joshi, T. (2020). "What others dare not say": An antisemitic conspiracy fantasy and its YouTube audience. *Journal of Contemporary Antisemitism*, *3*(1), 35–54. https://doi.org/10.26613/jca/3.1.42.

Ammerman, N. T. (2013). Spiritual but not religious? Beyond binary choices in the study of religion. *Journal for the Scientific Study of Religion*, *52*(2), 258–278. https://doi.org/10.1111/jssr.12024.

Anthony, L. (2021). AntConc (Version 3.5.8) [Computer software]. Tokyo: Waseda University.

Baker, P., Gabrielatos, C., & McEnery, T. (2013). *Discourse analysis and media attitudes: The representation of Islam in the British press*. Cambridge University Press.

Bamberg, M., & Georgakopoulou, A. (2008). Small stories as a new perspective in narrative and identity analysis. *Text & Talk*, *28*(3), 377–396. https://doi .org/10.1515/TEXT.2008.018.

Becci, I., Burchardt, M., & Giorda, M. (2017). Religious super-diversity and spatial strategies in two European cities. *Current Sociology*, *65*(1), 73–91.

Bhatt, I. (2023). *A semiotics of Muslimness in China*. Elements in Applied Linguistics. Cambridge University Press. www.cambridge.org/core/elements/ semiotics-of-muslimness-in-china/AB898053368AF49AC6A510385 CEFB1FD.

Bhatt, I., & Wang, H. (2023). Everyday heritaging: Sino-Muslim literacy adaptation and alienation. *International Journal of the Sociology of Language*, *2023*(281), 77–101. https://doi.org/10.1515/ijsl-2022-0058.

Blackledge, A., & Creese, A. (2020). Interaction ritual and the body in a city meat market. *Social Semiotics*, *30*(1), 1–24.

Blommaert, J., & Rampton, B. (2012). Language and superdiversity. MMG Working Paper 12–09. www.mmg.mpg.de/59855/wp-12-09.

Bredvik, L. S. (2020). *Discussing the faith: Multilingual and metalinguistic conversations about Religion* (Vol. 25). Walter de Gruyter.

Bruce, T. (2018). New technologies, continuing ideologies: Online reader comments as a support for media perspectives of minority religions. *Discourse, Context & Media, 24*, 53–75. https://doi.org/10.1016/j.dcm.2017.10.001.

Burchardt, M., & Becci, I. (2016). Religion and superdiversity: An introduction. *New Diversities, 18*(1), 1–7.

Butt, P. (2023). *Feminism, theology and everyday domestic skill within a phenomenological framework: An autoethnographic reflection.* Unpublished PhD thesis, University of Birmingham. http://etheses.bham.ac.uk//id/eprint/14576/.

Cameron, L. (2010). Metaphors and discourse activity. In L. Cameron & R. Maslen (Eds.), *Metaphor analysis: Research practice in applied linguistics, social sciences and the humanities* (pp. 3–25). Equinox.

Cameron, L. (2015). Embracing connectedness and change: A complex dynamic systems perspective for applied linguistic research. *AILA Review, 28*(1), 28–48.

Chilton, P., & Kopytowska, M. (2018). *Religion, language, and the human mind.* Oxford University Press.

Christens, B. D. (2010). Public relationship building in grassroots community organizing: Relational intervention for individual and systems change. *Journal of Community Psychology, 38*(7), 886–900. https://doi.org/10.1002/jcop.20403.

Clark, L., & Osborne, L. (2014, March 7). Islamist plot 'Operation Trojan Horse' to take over schools in Birmingham. *Daily Mail Online.* www.dailymail.co.uk/news/article-2575759/Revealed-Islamist-plot-dubbed-Trojan-Horse-string-schools-Birmingham-self-styled-Jihad.html.

Clift, R., & Helani, F. (2010). *Inshallah*: Religious invocations in Arabic topic transition. *Language in Society, 39*(3), 357–382. https://doi.org/10.1017/S0047404510000199.

Creese, A. (2008). Linguistic ethnography. In N. Hornberger (Ed.), *Encyclopedia of language and education* (Vol. 2, pp. 229–241). Springer.

Creese, A., & Blackledge, A. (2019). Translanguaging and public service encounters: Language learning in the library. *The Modern Language Journal, 103*(4), 800–814.

Crystal, D. (1965). *Linguistics, language, and religion.* Hawthorn Books.

De Fina, A., & Georgakopoulou, A. (2011). *Analyzing narrative: Discourse and sociolinguistic perspectives.* Cambridge University Press.

Deppermann, A. (2013). How to get a grip on identities-in-interaction: (What) does 'positioning' offer more than 'membership categorization'? Evidence from a mock story. *Narrative Inquiry, 23*(1), 62–88.

Dorst, A., & Klop, M.-L. (2017). Not a holy father: Dutch Muslim teenagers' metaphors for Allah. *Metaphor and the Social World, 7*(1), 65–85.

Fadil, N. (2017). Recalling the 'Islam of the parents': Liberal and secular Muslims redefining the contours of religious authenticity. *Identities*, *24*(1), 82–99. https://doi.org/10.1080/1070289X.2015.1091318.

Flores, N., & Lewis, M. (2016). From truncated to sociopolitical emergence: A critique of super-diversity in sociolinguistics. *International Journal of the Sociology of Language*, *2016*(241), 97–124. https://doi.org/10.1515/ijsl-2016-0024.

García, O., & Li, W. (2014). *Translanguaging and education*. Springer.

Georgakopoulou, A. (2006). Thinking big with small stories in narrative and identity analysis. *Narrative Inquiry*, *16*(1), 122–130.

Georgakopoulou, A. (2007). *Small stories, interaction and identities*. John Benjamins.

Gholami, R. (2015). *Secularism and identity: Non-Islamiosity in the Iranian diaspora*. Routledge.

Gholami, R. (2017). The art of self-making: Identity and citizenship education in late-modernity. *British Journal of Sociology of Education*, *38*(6), 798–811. https://doi.org/10.1080/01425692.2016.1182006.

Gholami, R. (2021). Critical race theory and Islamophobia: Challenging inequity in higher education. *Race Ethnicity and Education*, *24*(3), 319–337. https://doi.org/10.1080/13613324.2021.1879770.

Gilroy, P. (2004). *After empire*. Routledge.

Graeber, D. (2015). *The utopia of rules: On technology, stupidity, and the secret joys of bureaucracy*. Melville House.

Gregory, E., Choudhury, H., Ilankuberan, A., Kwapong, A., & Woodham, M. (2013). Practice, performance and perfection: Learning sacred texts in four faith communities in London. *International Journal of the Sociology of Language*, *2013*(220), 27–48. https://doi.org/10.1515/ijsl-2013-0012.

Hanks, W. F. (2013). Language in Christian conversion. In J. Boddy & M. Lambek (Eds.), *A companion to the anthropology of religion* (pp. 387–406). John Wiley and Sons.

Harré, R., & van Lagenhove, L. (1998). *Positioning theory: Moral contexts of intentional action*. Blackwell Publishers.

Hobbs, V. (2020). *An introduction to religious language: Exploring theolinguistics in contemporary contexts*. Bloomsbury Publishing.

Hogg, M. (2004). Social identity theory. In A. H. Eagly, R. M. Baron, & V. Hamilton (Eds.), *The social psychology of group identity and social conflict: Theory, application, and practice* (pp. 111–136). American Psychological Association.

Housley, W., & Fitzgerald, R. (2002). The reconsidered model of membership categorization analysis. *Qualitative Research*, *2*(1), 59–83.

Inge, A. (2016). *The making of a Salafi Muslim woman: Paths to conversion.* Oxford University Press.

Jackson, C. (2018, June 27). British white people set to become a minority in Birmingham, says report. *Birmingham Live.* https://bit.ly/2y5LiC8.

Jayyusi, L. (1984). *Categorization and the moral order.* Routledge/Kegan & Paul.

Jefferson, G. (1978). Sequential aspects of storytelling in conversation. In J. Schenkein (Ed.), *Studies in the organization of conversational interaction* (pp. 219–248). Academic Press. https://doi.org/10.1016/B978-0-12-623550-0.50016-1.

Labov, W. (1972). *Language in the inner city.* University of Pennsylvania Press.

Lytra, V., Volk, D., & Gregory, E. (2016). *Navigating languages, literacies and identities: Religion in young lives.* Routledge.

Noronha, L. de. (2022). The conviviality of the overpoliced, detained and expelled: Refusing race and salvaging the human at the borders of Britain. *The Sociological Review, 70*(1), 159–177. https://doi.org/10.1177/0038026121 1048888.

Office for National Statistics. (2022). How life has changed in Birmingham: Census 2021. www.ons.gov.uk/visualisations/censusareachanges/E08000025/.

Omoniyi, T., & Fishman, J. A. (2006). *Explorations in the sociology of language and religion.* John Benjamins Publishing Company.

Owen, W. F. (1984). Interpretive themes in relational communication. *Quarterly Journal of Speech, 70*(3), 274–287.

Pavlenko, A. (2018). Sloganization in language education discourse. In B. Schmenk, S. Breidbach, & L. Küster (Eds.), *Conceptual thinking in the age of academic marketization* (pp. 142–168). Multilingual Matters.

Pihlaja, S. (2014). 'Christians' and 'bad Christians': Categorization in atheist user talk on YouTube. *Text & Talk, 34*(5), 623–639.

Pihlaja, S. (2018). *Religious talk online: The evangelical discourse of Muslims, Christians, and atheists.* Cambridge University Press.

Pihlaja, S. (Ed.). (2021a). *Analysing religious discourse.* Cambridge University Press.

Pihlaja, S. (2021b). *Talk about faith: How conversation shapes belief.* Cambridge University Press.

Pihlaja, S. (2023). Abstraction in storytelling. *Narrative Inquiry.*

Pihlaja, S., & Ringrow, H. (Eds.). (2023). *The Routledge handbook of language and religion.* Routledge.

Pihlaja, S., Whisker, D., & Vickerage-Goddard, L. (2022). Categories in discourse about Church of England primary education. *Religion & Education, 49*(3), 292–309. https://doi.org/10.1080/15507394.2022.2102876.

Rampton, B., Tusting, K., Maybin, J., et al. (2012). UK linguistic ethnography: A discussion paper. www.lancaster.ac.uk/fss/organisations/lingethn/documents/discussion_paper_jan_05.pdf.

Richardson, P. (2012). A closer walk: A study of the interaction between metaphors related to movement and proximity and presuppositions about the reality of belief in Christian and Muslim testimonials. *Metaphor and the Social World*, *2*(2), 233–261.

Richardson, P., & Mueller, C. M. (2022). Contested paths: Analyzing unfolding metaphor usage in a debate between Dawkins and Lennox. *Metaphor and the Social World*, *12*(1), 138–158.

Richardson, P., Mueller, C., & Pihlaja, S. (2021). *Cognitive linguistics and religious language: An introduction*. Routledge.

Richardson, P., Pihlaja, S., Nagashima, M., et al. (2020). Blasphemy and persecution: Positioning in an inter-religious discussion. *Text & Talk*, *40*(1), 75–98. https://doi.org/10.1515/text-2019-2049.

Ringrow, H. (2020a). "Beautiful masterpieces": Metaphors of the female body in modest fashion blogs. In H. Ringrow & S. Pihlaja (Eds.), *Contemporary media stylistics* (pp. 15–34). Bloomsbury.

Ringrow, H. (2020b). "I can feel myself being squeezed and stretched, moulded and grown, and expanded in my capacity to love loudly and profoundly": Metaphor and religion in motherhood blogs. *Discourse, Context & Media*, *37*, 100429. https://doi.org/10.1016/j.dcm.2020.100429.

Ringrow, H. (2021). Identity. In S. Pihlaja (Ed.), *Analysing religious discourse* (pp. 276–291). Cambridge University Press.

Rosowsky, A. (2008). *Heavenly readings: Liturgical literacy in a multilingual context* (Vol. 9). Multilingual Matters.

Rosowsky, A. (2019). Sacred language acquisition in superdiverse contexts. *Linguistics and Education*, *53*, 100751. https://doi.org/10.1016/j.linged.2019.100751.

Rumsby, S., & Eggert, J. P. (2023). Religious positionalities and political science research in 'the field' and beyond: Insights from Vietnam, Lebanon and the UK. *Qualitative Research*, 14687941231165884. https://doi.org/10.1177/14687941231165884.

Rumsey, S. K. (2010). Faith in action: Heritage literacy as a synchronisation of belief, word and deed. *Literacy*, *44*(3), 137–143. https://doi.org/10.1111/j.1741-4369.2010.00561.x.

Sacks, H. (1992). *Lectures on conversation*. Blackwell.

Sierra, S. (2023). The epistemics of authentication and denaturalization in the construction of identities in social interaction. *Language in Society*, 52(4), 571–594. https://doi.org/10.1017/S0047404522000161.

Soskice, J. M. (1985). *Metaphor and religious language*. Oxford University Press.

Soskice, J. M. (2007). *The kindness of God: Metaphor, gender, and religious language*. Oxford University Press.

Souza, A. (2016). Language and faith encounters: Bridging language–ethnicity and language–religion studies. *International Journal of Multilingualism*, *13*(1), 134–148. https://doi.org/10.1080/14790718.2015.1040023.

Staples-Butler, J. (2020). Did a Corbyn-led government pose an "existential threat to Jewish life" in the UK? Revolutionary states and the destruction of Jewish communities. *Journal of Contemporary Antisemitism*, *3*(1), 109–120. https://doi.org/10.26613/jca/3.1.47.

Tajfel, H. (1983). *Social identity and intergroup relations*. Cambridge University Press.

Thompson, N., & Pihlaja, S. (2017). Young Muslims and exclusion – experiences of 'othering'. *Youth & Policy*. www.youthandpolicy.org/articles/young-muslims-and-exclusion/.

Translation and Translanguaging (TLANG). (n.d.). https://tlang.org.uk/.

Valluvan, S. (2016). Conviviality and multiculture: A post-integration sociology of multi-ethnic interaction. *YOUNG*, *24*(3), 204–221. https://doi.org/10.1177/1103308815624061.

van Noppen, J.-P. (1981). *Theolinguistics*. Studiereeks Tijdschrift Vrije Universiteit Brussel.

van Noppen, J.-P. (2006). From theolinguistics to critical theolinguistics: The case for communicative probity. *ARC, The Journal of the Faculty of Religious Studies*, *34*, 47–65.

van Noppen, J.-P. (2012). God in George W. Bush's rhetoric. https://o-re-la.ulb.be/analyses/item/175-god-in-george-w-bush%E2%80%99s-rhetoric.html.

Vertovec, S. (2007). Super-diversity and its implications. *Ethnic and Racial Studies*, *30*(6), 1024–1054.

Whisker, D., Pihlaja, S., & Vickerage-Goddard, L. (2020). *Diversity and success in church schools*. Grove Books.

Yee, E. (2019). Abstraction and concepts: When, how, where, what and why? *Language, Cognition and Neuroscience*, *34*(10), 1257–1265.

Yelle, R., Handman, C., & Lehrich, C. (Eds.). (2019). *Language and religion*. De Gruyter. https://doi.org/10.1515/9781614514329.

Cambridge Elements ☰

Applied Linguistics

Li Wei

University College London

Li Wei is Chair of Applied Linguistics at the UCL Institute of Education, University College London (UCL), and Fellow of Academy of Social Sciences, UK. His research covers different aspects of bilingualism and multilingualism. He was the founding editor of the following journals: *International Journal of Bilingualism* (Sage), *Applied Linguistics Review* (De Gruyter), *Language, Culture and Society* (Benjamins), *Chinese Language and Discourse* (Benjamins) and *Global Chinese* (De Gruyter), and is currently Editor of the *International Journal of Bilingual Education and Bilingualism* (Taylor and Francis). His books include the *Blackwell Guide to Research Methods in Bilingualism and Multilingualism* (with Melissa Moyer) and *Translanguaging: Language, Bilingualism and Education* (with Ofelia Garcia) which won the British Association of Applied Linguistics Book Prize.

Zhu Hua

University College London

Zhu Hua is Professor of Language Learning and Intercultural Communication at the UCL Institute of Education, University College London (UCL) and is a Fellow of Academy of Social Sciences, UK. Her research is centred around multilingual and intercultural communication. She has also studied child language development and language learning. She is book series co-editor for *Routledge Studies in Language and Intercultural Communication and Cambridge Key Topics in Applied Linguistics,* and Forum and Book Reviews Editor of *Applied Linguistics* (Oxford University Press).

About the Series

Mirroring the Cambridge Key Topics in Applied Linguistics, this Elements series focuses on the key topics, concepts and methods in Applied Linguistics today. It revisits core conceptual and methodological issues in different subareas of Applied Linguistics. It also explores new emerging themes and topics. All topics are examined in connection with real-world issues and the broader political, economic and ideological contexts.

Cambridge Elements ☰

Applied Linguistics

Elements in the Series

Printed in the United States
by Baker & Taylor Publisher Services